TAI
CHI
& the Daoist Spirit

An Anthology of Articles from the Journal of Asian Martial Arts
compiled by Michael A. DeMarco, M.A.

Disclaimer

Please note that the authors and publisher of this book are not responsible in any manner whatsoever for any injury that may result from practicing the techniques and/or following the instructions given within. Since the physical activities described herein may be too strenuous in nature for some readers to engage in safely, it is essential that a physician be consulted prior to training.

All Rights Reserved

Articles in this anthology were originally published in the *Journal of Asian Martial Arts*. Listed according to the table of contents for this anthology:

Holcombe, C. (1993), Vol. 2 No. 1, pp. 10-25
Willmont, D. (1997), Vol. 6 No. 1, pp. 10-29
DeMarco, M. (1997), Vol. 6 No. 3, pp. 8-17
Breslow, A. (1998), Vol. 7 No. 2, pp. 10-25
Hawthorne, M. (2000), Vol. 9 No. 1, pp. 70-81
Henning, S. (2007), Vol. 16 No. 3, pp. 22-25
Wile, D. (2007), Vol. 16 No. 4, pp. 8-45
Brodsky, G. (2012), 21 No. 1, pp. 82-101

Book and cover design
by Via Media Publishing Company

Edited by Michael A. DeMarco, M.A.

Cover illustrations

A gentleman atop the Great Wall and
taijii practice in Hangzhou, China.
Photos by M. DeMarco.

ISBN-13: 978-1893765467
ISBN-10: 1893765466

www.viamediapublishing.com

contents

preface

The eight chapters in this anthology present an encompassing perspective of how some Chinese martial art styles—and most significantly taijiquan—developed and evolved along with deep rooted traditions of spirituality and the quest for health and longevity. Much in this volume deals with Daoist theories and practices, particularly its influences ranging from human energetics (*qigong*) and other physical exercises (*daoyin*), to practical combative arts.

Holcombe, Willmont, and Breslow's well-researched chapters dive deeply into the philosophical, spiritual, and physical traditions associated with Daoism. The search for immortality is shown to be of prime importance since it gave impetus to the belief that human beings can live healthier, longer, and happier lives. My own chapter presents a way of directly discovering taijiquan's philosophical principles through experiential involvement in the art itself.

Henning's chapter gives an example in this tradition in the life of Ge Hong (284-363 CE). Known for his Daoist alchemical pursuits, Ge was also a military officer who provides valuable insights into Chinese martial arts practices.

Dr. Wile explores the ways in which martial arts have been exposed to cultural construction and deconstruction. A Daoist connection has figured in political ideology, national identity, and commercial interest during the past 400 years of Chinese history. The text focuses on the taijiquan as an important site of constructing "Chinese-ness."

From the early 20th century, the Chinese government often looked at Daoism as a form of superstition, and allowed temples to fall into disrepair. In the 21st century, as Hawthorne shows, there is a quest to rescue historic Daoist sites and study the tradition.

In the final chapter, Greg Brodsky applies a five-element yoga model to the practice of taijiquan as a "quality assurance test." It offers opportunities for deepening, enriching, and enjoying taiji practice.

In all, the chapters here offer insights for understanding how Chinese martial traditions—particularly taijiquan—developed and evolved within the framework of culture. "Taiji" takes on different meanings according to time and place. This also resolves the ongoing arguments regarding taijiquan as a practical combative art verses a health regimen. As a proverb points out: "From the standpoint of the sun, day and night have no meaning."

Michael A. DeMarco, Publisher
Santa Fe, New Mexico, October 2017

· 1 ·

The Daoist Origins
of the Chinese Martial Arts
by Charles Holcombe, Ph.D.

Daoist longevity exercises have greatly influenced China's martial art traditions. Here, an elderly gentleman strolls atop the Badaling section of the Great Wall. Long beards and the long wall are two of the many symbols for long life. *Photos by M. DeMarco.*

Some three decades ago Joseph Needham offered his opinion that "Chinese boxing... probably originated as a department of Taoist [Daoist] physical exercises."[1] This arresting hypothesis manages to strike us as both strange and yet oddly comfortable at the same time. We would expect that religion should have little to do with the deadly business of combat; yet, to anyone even remotely acquainted with the Chinese martial arts, the Daoist imprint is unmistakable. The present chapter is intended to explore the implications of this Daoist paternity. What exactly does it mean to say that the martial arts began with Daoist exercises, and what does that then tell us about the martial arts?

To begin with, it goes without saying that we do not intend to imply that the specific forms of the modern martial arts necessarily derive from older Daoist practices. What we do mean is simply that the basic philosophical underpinnings of the Chinese martial arts are Daoist. Beyond this, I venture to suggest that a technique which is central to the modern martial arts actually originated in Daoism. This technique is what has relatively recently come to be labeled qigong—*qi*, meaning breath or air, and *gong*, meaning achievement. The art has been defined by a contemporary Chinese scholar as "an active process of physical and mental discipline through the training of the heart/mind, the training of breathing, the training of the body and other means, which takes as its main goal the strengthening of human physical co-ordination."[2] In other words, it is the bending of qi to human intentions or "Daoist breath control."

Qigong has been surprisingly pervasive in Chinese thought. Even staid Confucians advocated its practice. Mencius (c. 372-279 BCE), for example, spoke of "cultivating my overwhelming qi," and in the twelfth century Zhu Xi (1130-1200) advocated the use of qigong breath control in his program of Neo-Confucian self-cultivation.[3] It is with the Daoist school, however, that the manipulation of the inner energies released by breath control is most intimately associated, and it was the Daoists who made the most extravagant claims for that technique. As the distinguished British Sinologist Arthur Waley put it, he who mastered Daoist breath control could "cure every disease, expose himself with immunity to epidemics, charm snakes and tigers, stop wounds from bleeding, stay under the water or walk upon it, stop hunger and thirst, and increase his own life-span."[4]

Such claims are fantastic. That they were, and sometimes still are, taken seriously can only be understood in the light of the Chinese scientific paradigm which took shape in the great eclectic *weltanschauung* of the Han dynasty (202 BCE-220 CE). This Han world-view envisioned the universe to be, in Derk Bodde's words, "a harmoniously functioning organism," the actions of whose component parts were each mutually related.[5] The complex interactions of yin and yang and five basic elements (*wuxing*) produced the manifold phenomena of nature. Elaborate sets of correlations were then devised for each element, and it was assumed that the correlates reacted sympathetically to each other.

This view is nicely illustrated in the following passage from the second century CE Daoist classic *Taiping Jing*:

> The nature of wood [one of the five elements] is humanity. If you con-
> template humanity, therefore, you will be transported to the East, since
> the East is the master of humanity. The five directions [including the
> center] are all like this. The affairs of the world all follow their own kind.
> Therefore, if emperors and kings think peacefully, their governments will
> be peaceful as well, through the appeal of likeness.[6]

Viewed through the lenses of "modern science," it is easy to dismiss the logical process in operation here as "thought magic," in Murakami Yoshimi's words, and rationalize its continued acceptance in otherwise sophisticated Imperial China as an anachronistic relic of more primitive times.[7] In fact, however, this was not "magic" as Sir James Frazer might have defined it, but a mechanical tool for eliciting action at a distance through direct cause and effect, by means of the correlations among the five elements, and physical contact through the universal environment of qi.

Nanjing Provincial Museum—a 2,000 year old jade burial suit made of nearly 2,600 squares of green jade. Such "jade cases" were only made for emperors and high-ranking aristocrats. Jade was often utilized in the making of weapons and clothing. Today, it remains a precious stone partly because it is associated with life-prolonging attributes.

Somewhat like the Western concept of the ether, qi was believed to be the substance surrounding and including all things, which brought even distant points into direct physical contact.[8] As the Liezi observed perhaps shortly after the fall of Han, "Heaven is merely amassed qi.... When you bend, stretch, or breath, you are always moving inside Heaven."[9]

Since one single substance joined all corners of the cosmos into a single organic unity, it followed that mastery of qi was equivalent to mastery of the material universe. The key was the mind. "What man can imagine, he can always bring about," says the *Taiping Jing*. "The mind and ideas are the pivotal mechanism of heaven and earth, and cannot be carelessly moved. If you cause harmonious ch'i [qi] to become disordered, calamities will occur daily."[10] It was seriously supposed that the words and actions of a properly cultivated gentleman could affect "places thousands of miles away," and in early imperial China, at least, such beliefs were not limited to so-called Daoists, but were shared by even such stolid Confucians as Fu Xuan (217-278), who pontificated that "the mind... is the controller of all things."[11]

The Han dynasty theoreticians were principally concerned about the implications of this discovery for government. It was supposed that the true ruler need only approach his task with a cultivated mind and settled heart for all the affairs of his domain to proceed in satisfactory harmony. But the ability of internal cultivation to transform external physical reality also had private significance, which in the long run proved to be of the greatest interest to most people. Specifically, proper circulation of qi could prolong one's life—perhaps indefinitely—and could enable the individual to accomplish otherwise incredible feats.

The technique of manipulating qi for personal satisfaction can be traced back at least as far as the late fifth century BCE, when it was referred to as "moving qi" (*xing qi*) on a jade pendant discovered recently by archaeologists.[12] The practice was evidently quite widespread even before the maturation of its theoretical explanation in the Han dynasty. According to the third century BCE Daoist classic *Zhuangzi*:

> Huffing and puffing, exhaling the old and inhaling the new, the bear pull and the bird stretch, is for long life and only that. This is what the gentlemen of Taoist [Daoist] exercises, men who nourish their bodies, and those who study the long life of P'eng Tsu [the "Chinese Methuselah"] like.[13]

Details of the jade burial suit on display in the Nanjing Provincial Museum.

By the Han dynasty the therapeutic physical exercises—Zhuangzi's "bear pull and bird stretch"—were called *daoyin*. Excellent illustrations of these daoyin exercises dating from the early Han were found in 1973 on silk scrolls unearthed at the tomb complex at Mawangdui.[14] The purpose of these exercises was to loosen up the circulatory system to permit the free passage of qi. As the first century CE skeptic Wang Chong wrote, Daoists "... suppose that if you do not shake, bend, and stretch the arteries in your body they will block up and not circulate, and if they do not circulate the accumulation will cause illness and death."[15]

Daoyin physical exercises were intended to facilitate the circulation of qi and were consequently secondary in importance to the actual manipulation of qi itself, which is often rendered in English as "breath control." This English term encompasses Zhuangzi's "huffing and puffing" without any problem but otherwise does not begin to do justice to the full range of the Chinese concept, since qi is not only breath but the very substance of the universe. Internally, within the human body, qi was envisioned as energy, often in fluid form.[16] When taken literally, as Daoist adepts so often did, this could be understood to mean saliva or the bodily fluids. According to one delightfully mystical text:

> The pure waters of the "jade pond" water the roots of the soul. If you investigate this and are able to cultivate it you can exist eternally. It is called "feeding upon nature." That which is natural is the "glorious pond." The "glorious pond" [refers to] the saliva in one's mouth. If you breathe in accordance with the rules and swallow it, you will not experience hunger.[17]

Such technologies were understood as ways to physically recycle, conserve, and nourish the bodily qi which the therapeutic daoyin exercises had cleared passages for. A late Han dynasty adept named Wang Chen, for example, "practiced shutting off his qi and swallowing it, calling it embryonic breathing, and swallowing [the fluid] coughed up from the spring beneath his tongue, calling it embryonic feeding."[18]

These early qigong practices may have focused on actual respiration or the circulation of bodily fluids, but mental concentration must have been a necessary concomitant of "breath control" from its inception. With time the role of the mind came to loom even larger. In fully evolved qigong practice the energy of qi is channeled through the body under mental impulse.[19] It was this mental activity, developed into a form of meditation known as "holding on to the one" (*shou-yi*) or "fixed thought" (*cun-si*), which actually unleashed the incredible powers of Daoist "breath control" noted by Arthur Waley.[20] Merely by thinking about it the adept can travel vast distances or cure diseases. As the *Baopuzi* recorded in the fourth century, "if you imagine the ch'i [qi] from your five internal organs emerging from your two eyes to surround your body like mist, ...you can then share a bed with the victim of a plague [without danger]."[21]

The arrival of Indian Buddhism in China shortly after the birth of Christ may have added a new current to the stream of Chinese meditative practice but probably did little more than refine an already existing Daoist tradition.[22] The Parthian monk An Shih-gao, for example, translated a Buddhist sutra on meditation through concentration on breathing (*anapana*) shortly after his arrival at the Han capital in 148 CE, but by that time concentrated thought was also a central fixture of the Daoist tradition as well.[23] The meditative aspect of qigong should, therefore, be considered essentially as part of the main Daoist line of transmission, even while acknowledging the possibility that there were important Buddhist contributions.[24]

Simplicity Embracing Monastery located on a hill overlooking
West Lake in Hangzhou city. It is noted as the place where
Daoist Ge Hong alchemically prepared elixirs for attaining immortality.

6

Some believe incense lifts prayers to heaven. In the Daoist tradition, individuals can also be found practicing various exercises for health and spiritual development. Some are obviously martial. Symbolically, incense can represent the movement of qi.

The meditative aspect of Daoist qigong in the Han dynasty is nicely illustrated by the following passage from the *Peng Zu ling*:

> Whoever moves his qi with the desire of eradicating the "hundred diseases" concentrates on wherever they are located. If his head aches he concentrates on his head, if his foot hurts he concentrates on his foot, combining his qi and sending it to attack it. In the time [the qi] takes to get there [the ache] will have dissipated by itself.[25]

Thus, although the term qigong had not yet been coined, qigong techniques were fully developed by the end of the Han dynasty. At the same time, true Daoist religion also emerged in the last century of the Han, and it soon absorbed and engulfed qigong. The new religion may have had distant precursors in shamanism, but its immediate ancestors are to be found among the *fangshi* ("gentlemen with prescriptions") who began to promote secret arts leading to immortality around the third century BCE.[26] Over the course of the next few centuries these arts evolved and spread until in the second century CE a man named Zhang Daoling (fl. c. 142) instigated a "religious revolution" by organizing a Daoist church dedicated to the pursuit of immortality.[27]

After a rather conventional beginning studying the classics, the story goes, Zhang had retired to a mountain in modern-day Sichuan to "study the Dao of long life."[28] With divine direction he obtained a sacred text which enabled him to fly and work various other miracles.[29] Because of his new ability to cure disease, "the common people thronged to him and served him as their teacher, the households of his disciples reaching the tens of thousands."[30]

The new faith struck a responsive chord in late Han China, and the quest for immortality soon became all the rage among the elite. In the second century the *Taiping Jing* claimed, perhaps with some hyperbole, that "the perfect gentlemen of the empire eschew office for immortality."[31] After the fall of Han, Chi Yin (313-384)—who strolled about with friends, "settled his heart, stopped eating grain, and cultivated the [Daoist] arts of Huang-Lao [the Yellow Emperor and Laozi]"—was typical of the lofty literati who dominated the era of division that followed.[32] Even Buddhism flourished in the immediate post-Han era largely "as a religion of immortal recipes."[33]

The medieval immortality cult was eclectic and borrowed from every conceivable tradition, including Daoist breath control. Of the adepts (still referred to here as *fangshi*) at the court of the Wei Kingdom early in the third century CE, for example, "[Kan] Shih is able to move his ch'i [*qi*] and perform tao-yin [daoyin] exercises, [Tso] Tz'u is enlightened about the [sexual] arts 'within the chamber,' and [Xi] Chien is good at avoiding [eating] grains. They all claim to be three hundred years old."[34] A text called the *Lai Xiang li*, which may date from the fourth century, listed no fewer than thirty-six different methods for nourishing one's nature and attaining immortality, ranging from "breathing and visualizing the cinnabar field" to "using sacrifices to bring spirits" and eremitism.[35] Qigong mixed freely with cabalistic ideas and talismanic beliefs: the medieval Daoists "also make seals of wood, engraving stars, planets, the sun and moon upon them; and, inhaling ch'i [*qi*] and grasping them, they use them to seal a disease, curing many."[36]

In the Han and pre-Han periods qigong had enjoyed a preeminent position among the arts of longevity. When asked for the secret of his long life by Emperor Wen early in the second century BCE, for example, the 180-year-old Duke Dou supposedly replied: "Your servant [practices] tao-yin [*daoyin*]; it is not that I have taken any potions."[37] In the immortality cult that flowered after the fall of the Han, however, it was the elixir of immortality which eclipsed qigong.[38]

Chinese elixirs apparently originated with the shaman's use of intoxicants in antiquity to induce trances. The drugs used for that purpose may have included alcohol, hallucinogenic mushrooms, and other less well-defined "medicines."[39] The *Shan Hai ling*, for example, speaks of a mountain where no fewer than ten shamans "rise and descend, gathering the hundred medicines."[40] This use of drugs was then picked up and elaborated on by the *fangshi* of the early Imperial era, and emerged as the path of choice to immortality in the third century CE.

The ingredients of medieval immortality potions included fungi and something known as the "five mineral" powder.[41] Gold was another favorite substance. With typical literal-mindedness some Daoists reasoned that since "it is in the nature of gold that it does not decay.... [so, too,] when the alchemist consumes it he obtains immortality."[42] However, it was the "refinement of cinnabar" (*lian-dan*) that was most esteemed by serious adherents of the immortality cult. Cinnabar (HgS, or mercuric sulfide), in fact, came to be a veritable synonym for the elixir itself, and it was in the shadow of that mighty potion that by the sixth century qigong came to be known as *neidan*, or "internal cinnabar," in self-conscious imitation of the more important "external cinnabar" (*waidan*) which was the elixir of immortality itself.[43]

It may strike the reader as odd that intelligent literati were so credulous as to believe in physical immortality. Not all were, but China did have a long tradition of belief in ancestral spirits, ghosts, and other such things. In this the Chinese cannot be said to have been any more credulous than other peoples, but the Chinese were also "rational" enough to question whether it was possible for spirits to exist apart from the material world. Prior to the introduction of the Buddhist belief in reincarnation, therefore, many Chinese suspected that at death "the body and spirit were extinguished together" or at least that their residue was transformed into new material objects.[44] A non-corporeal immortality of the soul in the Christian sense was simply inconceivable, but, this did not mean that spirits did not exist.[45] Like the air itself, which was also composed of physical matter, they were ethereal but physical beings invisible to mortal eyes.[46]

"Immortals" (*xian*), then, were simply deathless spiritual beings who belonged to a more rarefied sphere of matter than mankind.[47] Since all objects in the universe were constructed of a single basic substance, and since all things were in a constant process of transformation, it followed that almost anything could theoretically be transformed into almost anything else if only the necessary preconditions could be met.[48] As Tung Jung-chang (179-219) wrote, "Those who attain the Tao [*Dao*] sprout pinions on their arms, long feathers on their bellies, fly the unscalable blue sky, and pass over the interminable affairs of this world."[49] Medicine seemed a reasonable catalyst for this change, moreover, since the relentless Han expectation of natural symmetry implied that if there were drugs that could kill people, as there certainly were, there should also be corresponding drugs that were antidotes for death.[50]

Unfortunately, the medicines that medieval alchemists brewed often proved harmful or fatal to those who consumed them.[51] It was not unnatural, under the circumstances, for skeptics to point to the absence of evidence for success and wonder, if it were really possible to attain immortality, where all the immortals were.[52]

In his "Essay on Nourishing Life" (*Yang Sheng Lun*), Xi Kang (223-262) began cautiously:

> In this world there are those who say that immortality can be obtained through study, and that through effort one can avoid death. There are others who say that a maximum age of 120 has been the same in antiquity and modern times, and that going beyond this is always a fantastic delusion. Both of these [positions] neglect the facts. [53]

For Xi the records of immortals in the old histories were proof enough that immortals had actually existed, but he then went on to suggest that they must have been "specially endowed with a different" qi. For modern man to attain immortality, while still theoretically within the realm of possibility, was practically out of reach. Instead, Xi's recipe for nourishing life in the modern world was simply to harmonize with the Dao, consume medicines and drink wine, and nestle into calm inactivity. "Forget enjoyment, and then your pleasure will be sufficient. Neglect life, and then your body will be preserved."[54] In the classic Daoist paradox, since the Dao works through a process of reversal, "those who do not treat life as valuable are the ones who excel at valuing life."[55]

Although Xi Kang did believe in immortals and was actually one of the more prominent third century enthusiasts for collecting medicines and methods of mental and physical self-cultivation, he also clearly possessed a healthy dose of skepticism and had a realistic sense of the possibilities.[56] In the sixth century, Xi's caution was echoed by Yan Chi-dui (531-591), who advised his sons to avoid the futile search for immortality but conceded that nourishing the spirit, breath control, and the proper use of medicine could result in longer life.[57]

The most ardent seekers of immortality were apologetic. In the second century, the *Taiping Jing* warned that" [some] doctors and shamans only want to get people's money."[58] The royal family of third century Wei, who had summoned an assortment of *fangshi* to their court, explained that, of course, "we all consider this to be laughable and do not put any credence in it."[59] And in the most famous of all collections of formulas for immortality, the author of the fourth century *Baopuzi* protested with evident embarrassment that he only wanted "to treat the logic in things exhaustively."[60]

With the waning of the medieval social order after the late Tang dynasty (618-907), the immortality cult gradually diminished in importance. Internal self-cultivation through qigong, often referred to during this period as *neidan*, largely superseded the consumption of elixirs.[61] The mainstream of elite scholar-official interest in the late Imperial period was diverted away from overt religious enthusiasms towards secular Neo-Confucianism, but the religious nimbus surrounding qigong spread now to China's common people through the rise of new forms of popular sectarian Buddho-Daoist religion.

The most famous of these sects was called the White Lotus Society. This sect claimed to have been founded in the era of division after the fall of the Han, but actually seems not to have reached mature form until as late as the sixteenth century.[62] For our purposes the significant thing about White Lotus sectarian religion is that it taught qigong as part of its repertoire of salvationist techniques.[63] It was out of societies like the White Lotus—if not the White Lotus sect itself—that the historical Chinese martial arts first appeared.

No better illustration of the martial arts in practice can be found than the Boxer uprising that erupted at the beginning of the twentieth century. The reason this is such a fascinating example is that the Boxers' so-called "boxing" really consisted of shamanistic dances for inducing spiritual possession and divine invincibility, and not the kind of martial arts combat we would expect.[64] Nor were the Boxers unique in this respect. In many less well-known martial associations as well, such as the early twentieth century Red Spears studied by Elizabeth Perry, ritual magic seems to have been the most prominent feature.[65] The simple explanation for this is that in premodern China "martial arts" were part of a larger matrix of religious belief and practice and inseparable from that religious context.

In the twentieth century, however, "science" and "democracy" became the new watchwords for educated Chinese youth. During the "New Culture"· and "May Fourth" movements that began in World War I, the Chinese intelligentsia attempted to remake completely Chinese culture in the Western image. Old religious practices were denounced as "superstition" and rejected as embarrassing reminders of China's backward feudal past.

Qigong was not discarded during this century of modernization, but it was stripped of its burden of religious "superstition." Today qigong is presented as a part of China's lengthy folk medical tradition.[66] It is now considered a "scientific" rather than a religious technique for curing diseases and lengthening life, and, like so much of China's native medical tradition, it is currently attracting worldwide interest. Exciting, if as yet unverified, successes have been reported in treating such fashionable diseases as cancer using qigong.[67]

It is certainly not an error to treat qigong as a medical technology in this fashion. In the fourth century BCE *Inner Classic of the Yellow Emperor*, for example, the daoyin and xingqi forms of qigong were already listed as varieties of medical treatment alongside moxabustion, massage, acupuncture, and the consumption of drugs.[68] A Daoist adept in the third century southern state of Wu "fasted to await the patient's cure whenever he moved his ch'i [*xingqi*] to treat someone's illness."[69] A sixth-century bibliographic treatise in the *Sui shu* even mentions a short book in one scroll, "On Methods of Treatment with Qi" (*Lun qi chi liao fang*).[70] In the medieval immortality cult, however, the healing of diseases was but the first step in a continuum that led eventually to immortality. No clear separation was even conceivable between medicine and religion.

It was out of this same religious matrix that the modern martial arts emerged. The fighter and the healer are bound together by their common religious background and by their shared technology of qigong. Many of the popular martial art forms in late Imperial China, such as taijiquan (supreme ultimate boxing), xingiquan (body and thought boxing), and baguachang (eight trigrams hands), show clear evidence of qigong influence.[71] Taiji in particular is interesting. It is the quintessential Chinese martial art, but its practice is marked by breath control, concentration, and graceful dance-like movements. The casual Western observer might never even guess that it was supposed to be a form of combat. And yet the experts all insist it is the most deadly martial art of all.[72] If so, this may be because concentration of the kind developed in qigong really is a way to better health, coordination, and keener combat ability. As the Han dynasty thinkers had realized long ago, the mind really can be the key to many things.

Notes

1 J. Needham, *Science and Civilization in China, Vol. 2* (Cambridge: Cambridge University Press, 1962), 145-6. See also Wang Hsinwu, *T'ai chi ch'üan-fa ching-i* (The Essential Meaning of the Methods of Taijiquan) (Hong Kong: T'aip'ing shuchü, 1962), l.

2 Li Chih-yung, ed., *Chung-kuo ch'i-kung shih* (A History of Chinese Qigong) (Honan: Honan k'o-hsüeh chi-shu ch'upanshe, 1988), 2.

3 *Meng Tzu* (Mencius), annotated by Chao Ch'i (Ssu-pu ts'ung-kan edition; Shanghai: Shanghai shang-wu yin-shu-kuan, 1929), 3.6b. For Zhu Xi, see Li Chih-yung, 26.

4 A. Waley, *The Way and its Power: A Study of the Tao Te Ching and its Place in Chinese Thought* (Guilford: Billing and Sons, Ltd., 1934), 118.

5 D. Bodde, "The Chinese cosmic magic known as watching for the ethers," *Essays on Chinese Civilization* (Princeton: Princeton University Press, 1981), 351-52.

6 *T'ai-p'ing ching ho-chiao* (The Collated Classic of Great Peace), ed. by Wang Ming (Peking: Chunghua shuchü, 1960), 27.

7 Murakami Yoshimi, *Chogoku no sennin–Hobokushi no shiso* (Chinese Immortals–The Thought of the Pao-p'u tzu) (Kyoto: Heirakuji shoten, 1956), 139.

8 See C. Le Blanc, *Huai Nan Tzu: Philosophical Synthesis in Early Han Thought* (Hong Kong: Hong Kong University Press, 1985), 204; K. DeWoskin, *A Song for One or Two: Music and the Concept of Art in Early China*, Michigan Papers in Chinese Studies, No. 42 (Ann Arbor: University of Michigan Center for Chinese Studies, 1982), 38.

9 *Lieh tzu*, annotated by Chang Chan (c. 340-400) (reprint; Taipei: Taiwan chung-hua shuchü, 1982), 1.14a.

10 *T'ai-p'ing ching*, 25, 311.

11 For the words of the gentleman, see Wu Luchiang and Tenney Davis, tr., "An Ancient Chinese Treatise on Alchemy Entitled Ts'an T'ung Ch'i," *Isis*, 18.2 (1932), 245. Fu Xuan's text on "Rectifying the Mind" is included in *Ch'üan Chin wen* (Complete Writings of the Qin Dynasty), in *Ch'üan shang-ku san-tai Ch'in Han san-kuo liu-ch'ao wen*, ed. by Yen K'o-chün (1762-1843) (reprint; Kyoto: Chobun shuppansha, 1981), 1733.

12 Li Chih-yung, 9. Murakami Yoshimi defines *xingqi* as "to take in much ch'i [qi] and breathe deeply"(2).

13 *Chuang tzu tsuan-chien* (The Annotated Zhuangzi), ed. by Ch'ien Mu (Hong Kong: Tung-nan yin-wu ch'upanshe, n.d.), 122. *The Inner Classic of the Yellow Emperor* (Huangti neiching) also contains important early references to

qigong, and may be somewhat older. Francis Ruey-shuang Lee suggests it may date from the fourth century BCE. (*The "Silent Art" of Ancient China: Historical Analysis of the Intellectual and Philosophical Influences in the Earliest Medical Corpus Ling Shu Ching* [Taipei: Linking Publishing Co., 1980], 46).

14 Lin Hou-sheng and Lo P'ei-yü, *Chi-kung san-pai wen* (Three Hundred Questions Concerning Qigong) (Canton: Kuang-tung k'o-chi ch'upanche, 1983), 5.

15 Wang Ch'ung (27-c. 100 CE), *Lun Heng* (An Appraisal of Discussions) (reprint; Taipei: Taiwan chunghua shuchü, 1981), 7.19b.

16 See Ishida Hidemi, "Body and mind: The Chinese perspective," in *Taoist Meditation and Longevity Techniques*, ed. by L. Kohn (Ann Arbor: Center for Chinese Studies, University of Michigan, 1989), 45.

17 *Huang-t'ing ching* (The Classic of the Yellow Court), quoted in T'ao Hung-ching (456-536 CE), *Yang-hsingyen-ming lu* (A record of cultivating nature and prolonging life), in *Tao-tsangyang-sheng shu shih-chung*, ed. by Li Shih-hua and Shen Te-hui (Peking: Chung-i ku-chi ch'upanshe, 1987), 5.

18 *Ts'e-ju yüan-keui* (The Great Tortoise of the Archives) (c. 1013) (reprint; Taipei: Taiwan chunghua shuchü, 1981), 836.9917.

19 The importance of thought in qigong is eloquently stated in Miura Kunio, "The revival of Qi: Qigong in contemporary China," in L. Kohn, ed., *Taoist Meditation*, 337.

20 Murakami Yoshimi, 147. Daoist concentration is described in Li Chihyung, 96 ff.

21 Ko Hung (c. 280-340), *Pao-p'u tzu* (The Master Embracing Simplicity) (reprint; Taipei: Taiwan chung-hua shuchü, 1984), nei-p'ien 15.7a-8a.

22 Chang Chung-yuan ("An introduction to Taoist yoga," *The Review of Religion*, 20.3-4 [1956]) tentatively asserts the relative priority of indigenous Chinese techniques.

23 For An Shih-gao, see Tsukamoto Zenryu, "The early stages in the introduction of Buddhism into China (Up to the fifth century A.D.)," *Cahiers d'histoire mondials*, 5.3 (1960), 557.

24 The modern martial arts are often closely associated with Buddhism especially through the Shaolin school in China and Zen in Japan—but this is actually a perversion of the important Buddhist belief in pacifism and can be explained in part as a result of a strong Daoist influence. See P.l Demieville, "Le bouddhisme etla guerre, " *Choix d'etudes bouddhiques* (Leiden: E.J. Brill, 1973), 288 and passim.

25 *P'eng Tsu ching* (The classic of Peng Zi), in *Yang-hsing yen-ming lu*, 14. The text is ascribed to the late Han by C. Despeux, "Gymnastics: The ancient

tradition," in L. Kohn, ed., *Taoist Meditation*, 229.

[26] A link between these *fangshi* and the older practices of shamanism has been observed by Li Feng-mao ("Fu-Ch'u-tz'u te k'ao-ch'a chih-i" [Personal Adornment, the Consumption of Medicine, and Shamanistic Tradition: An Investigation of the *Ch'u Tz'u* from the Perspective of Shamanism], Ku-tienwenhsüeh, 3 [1981], 89) and others. For shamanism, see E. Harvey, "Shamanism in China," *Studies in the Science of Society*, ed. by G.Murdock (New Haven: Yale University Press, 1937). For the rise of *fangshi*, see Ku Ming-chien (Ku Chieh-kang), Ch'in Han te fang-hih yü ju-sheng (Qin and Han fangshi and Confucians) (1933; Taipei: Li-jen shuchü, 1985), 11. Ssuma Ch'ien (145-90 BCE) ascribed the deceits of *fangshi* to a misunderstanding of the scientific principle of the succession of yin and yang. See *Shih-chi* (Records of the Grand Historian) (Peking: Chunghua shuchü, 1959), 1368-69.

[27] M. Strickmann, "On the alchemy of T'ao Hung-ching," in *Facets of Taoism: Essays in Chinese Religion*, ed. by H. Welch and A. Seidel (New Haven: Yale University Press, 1979), 165.

[28] *T'ai-p'ing kuang-chi* (Extensive Records of the Taiping Era), ed. by Li Fang (925-996) (reprint; Peking: Chunghua shuchü, 1981), 55-56.

[29] *Yü-chih-t'ang t'an-hui* (Clustered Conversations of the Jade and Iris Hall), ed. by Hsü Yün-lin (fl. c. 1616) (1875 edition), 17.21a.

[30] *T'ai-p'ing kuang-chi*, 56.

[31] *T'ai-p'ing ching*, 403.

[32] Yu-chün nien-p'u (A Chronicle of the General of the Right), ed. by Lu I-t'ung, Mei-shu ts'ung-shu 4.9 (1855; Taipei: I-wen yin-shu-kuan, n.d.), 370.

[33] Tsukamoto Zenryu, *Shina bukkyoshi kenkyo, hoku-Gi hen* (Studies in the History of Chinese Buddhism, the Northern Wei Chapters) (Tokyo: Kobunto shobo, 1942), 49.

[34] Ch'en Shou (233-97), *San-kuo shih* (The Annals of the Three Kingdoms) (Peking: Chunghua shuchü, 1959), 29.805.

[35] This text is quoted in *Ch'u-hsüeh chi* (A Record for Initial Study), edited by Hsü Chien (659-729) (reprint; Peking: Chunghua shuchü, 1962), 23.54950. The work is otherwise unknown and undatable, but Lai-hsiang was a place name in the Qin dynasty.

[36] Wei Cheng (580-643), ed., *Sui-shu* (History of the Sui Dynasty) (reprint; Peking: Chunghua shuchü, 1973), 35.1093.

[37] Huan T'an (43 BCE-28CE), *Huan tzu hsin-lun* (New essays of Master Huan) (reprint; Taipei: Taiwan chunghua shuchü, 1976), 11b. Different versions of

the story are in circulation.

[38] According to Murakami Yoshimi (143), spiritual immortality could be attained by union with the Dao through meditation, but immortality of the body required the consumption of medicines, swallowing qi, and so on.

[39] See Chang Kwang-chih, *Art, myth, and ritual: The path to political authority in ancient China* (Cambridge: Harvard University Press, 1983), 55; M. Strickmann, *Notes on mushroom cults in ancient China* (Ghent: Rijksuniversiteit, 1966).

[40] *Shan hai ching chiao-chu* (The collated and annotated Classic of Mountains and Seas) (date uncertain), ed. by Yüan K'o (Shanghai: Shanghai kuchi ch'upanshe, 1980), 16.396.

[41] Chang Hua (232-300), *Po-wu chih* (An account of diverse phenomena) (reprint; Taipei: Taiwan chunghua shuchü, 1983), 7.1b. The so-called "five mineral powder" is discussed in Kuo Lin-ko, "Wei Chin feng-liu" (The fashions of the Wei and Chin), *Chungkuo hsüeh-pao*, 1.6 (1944), 48.

[42] *Ts'an t'ung ch'i k'ao-i* (An examination of variants in the covenant of the union of the three) (c. 142), ed. by Zhu Xi (reprint; Taipei: Taiwan chunghua shuchü, 1983), 12a.

[43] For the appearance of the term *neidan*, see Ko Chao-kuang, *Tao-chiao yü chungkuo wenhua* (Daoism and Chinese culture), Chungkuo wenhua shih ts'ung-shu (Shanghai: Shanghai jenmin ch'upanshe, 1987), 110. Isabelle Robinet ("Original contributions of neidan to Taoism and Chinese thought," in Kohn, ed., *Taoist meditation*, 301) limits the designation *neidan* to only those texts actually using chemical terminology, but clearly the comparison with laboratory alchemy helped shape the identity of qigong practice in general during this period.

[44] Cheng Tao-tzu (5th century), "Shen pu mieh lun" (On the Non-Extinction of the Spirit), contained in *Hungming chi* (The Collection Expanding Illumination), ed. by Seng Yu (435.518) (reprint; Taipei: Taiwan chunghua shuchü, 1983), 5.2a. Cheng, of course, argues for the Buddhist position. For a classic description of the process of death, see *Lieh tzu*, 1.9b.

[45] D. Holzman (*La vie et la pensee de Hi K'ang* [223.262 Ap. J.-C.] [Leiden: E. J. Brill, 1957], 53) observes that for the third century Chinese "une immortalite sans le corps est impensable [immortality with the body is unthinkable]. "

[46] The discussant in Hui-yüan's (334-416) "Sha-men pu ching wang che lun" (Sramana are Not Those Who Honor Kings) (*Hung ming chi*, 5.9a) offers the apparently trite opinion that "although the spirit is a subtle thing, it is certainly still something that is transformed by yin and yang." As much as

the coarsest of substances, spirits too were part of the physical world.

[47] See N. Sivin, *Chinese Alchemy: Preliminary Studies* (Cambridge: Harvard University Press, 1968), 41; Yü Ying-shih, "Life and immortality in the mind of Han China," *Harvard Journal of Asiatic Studies*, 25 (1965), 88-89.

[48] See H. Dubs, "The Beginnings of Alchemy, " *Isis*, 38.1-2 (1947), 73, note 76. The third century understanding of fundamental unity amid constant change is noted, for example, in I. Robinet, "Kouo Siang ou le monde comme absolu," *T'oung Pao*, 69.1-3 (1983), 83.

[49] *Ch'üan Hou Han wen* (Complete Writings of the Later Han Dynasty), in *Ch'üan shang-ku san-tai Ch'in Han san-kuo liu-ch'ao wen*, 89.955.

[50] The skeptic Huan Tan was told that since "Heaven produced medicines that kill men, there must be medicines to make men live" (*Huan tzu hsin-lun*, 26a.) Huan's astute reply was that poisons are not actually medicines to kill people, but rather substances which are simply not appropriate to eat.

[51] The effects of taking these drugs have been thoroughly studied in Ho Ping-yü and J. Needham, "Elixir poisoning in medieval China," *Janus, 48* (1959).

[52] See Xiang Xiu's third century criticism of Xi Kang, translated in Robert G. Henricks, *Philosophy and Argumentation in Third-Century China: The Essays of Hsi K'ang* (Princeton: Princeton University Press, 1983), 35.

[53] *Ch'üan san-kuo wen* (Complete writings of the Three Kingdoms), in *Ch'üan shang-ku san-tai Ch'in Han san-kuo liu-ch'ao wen*, 48.1324.

[54] Ibid., 48.1324-25.

[55] *Chin-shu* (History of the Qin Dynasty), ed. by Fang Hsüan-ling (578. 648) (reprint; Peking: Chunghua shuchü, 1974), 49.1370.

[56] Xi's thought is discussed in Horiike Nobuo, "Kei Ko ni okeru shinko to shakai: Sho Shu to no 'yojoron' ronso o chushin to shite" (Faith and Society in Xi Kang–Centering on the Debate with Xiang Xiu over his "Essay on Nourishing Life") *Rekishi ni okeru minshu to bunka: Sakai Tadao sensei koki shukuga kinen ronshu* (Tokyo: Kokusho kankokai, 1982), 109; Holzman, 52.60; and Li Fengmao, "Hsi K'ang yang-sheng ssu-hsiang chih yen-chiu" (Studies of Xi Kang's thought on nourishing life), *Ching-i wen-li hsüeh-yüan hsüeh-pao, 2* (1979).

[57] Yen Chih-t'ui [Yan Chi-dui], *Family Instructions for the Yen Clan: Yenshih chia-hsün*, trans., by Teng Ssu-yü (Leiden: E.J. Brill, 1968), 131-133.

[58] *T'ai-p'ing ching*, 620.

[59] *San-kuo chih*, 29.805.

[60] Ko Hung, *Alchemy, Medicine and Religion in the China of A.D. 320: The Nei P'ien of Ko Hung*, trans. by J. Ware (Dover, 1966), 206.

[61] See N. Sivin, "Science and medicine in Imperial China—The state of the field," *Journal of Asian Studies*, 47.1 (1988), 55. This movement parallels the simultaneous philosophical shift from Daoist concepts of external transcendence back towards Buddhist and Confucian themes of the immanence of truth within oneself. See Mori Mikisaburo, "Chogoku shiso ni okers choetsu to naizai" (Transcendence and Immanence in Chinese Thought), *Toyo gakujutsu kenkyu*, 23.2 (1984), 124.

[62] For an overview of White Lotus sectarianism, see Susan Naquin, "The transmission of White Lotus sectarianism in late imperial China," in *Popular Culture in Later Imperial China*, ed. by D. Johnson, et al. (Berkeley: University of California Press, 1985).

[63] The use of qigong in the White Lotus movement is described in D. Overmeyer, *Folk Buddhist Religion: Dissenting Sects in Late Traditional China* (Cambridge: Harvard University Press, 1976), 188, 190-92; Naquin, 275.

[64] See Kobayashi Kazumi, "Giwandan no minsho shiso" (The popular thought of the boxers), in *Koza Chogoku kingendai-shi 2: Giwandan undo* (Tokyo: Tokyo daigaku shuppankai, 1978), 243.

[65] E. Perry, *Rebels and Revolutionaries in North China, 1845-1945* (Stanford: Stanford University Press, 1980), 186-197.

[66] See Linda Chih-ling Koo, *Nourishment of Life: The Culture of Health in Traditional Chinese Society* (Ph.D. dissertation, University of California; Ann Arbor: University Microfilms, 1976), 71-72. Lin Hou-sheng (1), for example, introduces qigong as one of China's folk medical practices.

[67] Cui Lili ("Fitness and health through qigong," *Beijing Review* 32.1 7 [April 24-30, 1989]: 20, 22) reports that qigong has successfully been used to treat "terminal cancer patients" in the People's Republic. It is not clear yet how credible such claims are.

[68] *Ling-shu ching* (The classic of the spiritual axis), in *Huang-ti su-wen ling-shu ching* (The Yellow Emperor's Classics of Common Questions and the Spiritual Axis), annotated by Wang Ping (Ssu-pu ts'ung-k'an edition; Shanghai: Shang-hai shang-wu yin-shu-kuan, 1929), 7.3a.

[69] *Pao-p'u tzu, nei-p'ien* 15.3a.

[70] *Sui-shu*, 34.1046.

[71] See Li Chih-yung, 392. N. Sivin ("Science and Medicine," 68) notes real differences between taijiquan and the ancient daoyin exercises, however.

[72] For the effectiveness of taijiquan in martial arts competition, see "Fang t'ai-chi ta-shih Wang P'ei-sheng), *Jenmin jih-pao* (People's Daily), overseas edition, Aug. 3, 1987, 2.

18

· 2 ·

Sacrifice, Ritual, & Alchemy:
Spiritual Traditions in Taijiquan
by Dennis Willmont, L.Ac.

"Wave Hands Like Clouds."
Photograph courtesy of M. DeMarco.

Philosophical Background of Taijiquan

Taijiquan is an internal martial art known for its emphasis on mental and spiritual development. It is further characterized as a predetermined sequence of movements performed in slow motion. Thus, taijiquan is set apart from other martial arts whose movements are always performed at fast speed, as well as forms of sitting meditation and contemplation that place much less emphasis on the body. In contrast to dance as a performing art, which connects to the world externally through the interpersonal and horizontal communication between the artist and his or her audience, taijiquan connects to the world internally through a vertical communication between matter and spirit or, as in the Chinese manner, between heaven and earth (*tian di*). Communication between the heavenly and earthly poles of existence has been of paramount importance to the Chinese throughout their long history, of which taijiquan is but a comparatively recent development.

Although legends say taijiquan was created by Zhang Sanfeng in the Song Dynasty (960-1278 CE), its philosophical roots go back to the beginning of recorded history in China encompassing the development of Chinese thought as well as men's relation to one another and the natural universe. These roots include ancestor and spirit worship in the Shang Dynasty (1766-1154 BCE), the development of Confucianism in the Zhou Dynasty (1122-255 BCE), the origination of Daoism in the Warring States period (403-222 BCE), the development of alchemy in the Han Dynasty (206 BC-189 CE), and beyond. To understand important concepts in taijiquan, such as *xu* (emptiness), *wuwei* (effortlessness), and *zuran* (spontaneity), as well as the internal purpose of taijiquan itself (i.e., connecting to the source of the universe within the core of one's being), it is necessary to view taijiquan in this cultural and historical context.

To begin with, the very name "taijiquan" denotes a process that is simultaneously physical, mental, and spiritual. The word *quan* etymologically depicts a hand (*shou*) flexing (*quan*) into a fist (Weiger, 1965: 710). Superficially, this refers to taijiquan as a style, but on a deeper level *quan* refers to the embodiment of the spiritual and philosophical realms, i.e., "grasping" the relevance and deeper meaning inherent in the term "taiji."

"Taiji," or Great Ridgepole (sometimes called Great Ultimate), is a very ancient philosophical term referring to the gateway to the universe's origin. The term "taiji" first appears in the Great Appendix of the *Yijing* (Book of Changes), where eight stages are described in the creation of the physical world. According to the *Yijing*, taiji (stage 1) is what produces the two principles (*yi*) of yin and yang (stage 2) from the Great Void, which is considered the nondifferentiated, empty (*xu*) source (*yuan*) of all things (stage 0). Yin and yang, then, begin an energetic process of interpenetration and incubation through which the physical embryo is fashioned and birth takes place. The third stage produces the first level of this interpenetration in what are called the "Four Symbols" (*si xiang*), which describe this interpenetration in four different polar aspects: yin, yang, yin within yang, and yang within yin. The following four stages describe this continuing interpenetration in more detail. To avoid the confusion that would result by naming each of these stages according to the linguistics of yin and yang, especially on the seventh level, where there are six levels of yin-yang interpenetration, more easily understood visual symbols were used by ancient philosophers instead. Thus, this yin-yang interpenetration was conveyed by them through a system of solid and broken lines, in which the solid lines represented yang and the broken lines represented yin. Stage four resulted in eight different groups of three-lined symbols called the eight trigrams. Stage seven resulted in sixty-four different groups of six-lined symbols called the sixty-four hexagrams (Sung, 1935: 229).[1] Each trigram and each hexagram was further associated with names and symbols derived from the natural and social worlds. In this way, they were more readily distinguished from one another. The trigrams were named according to symbols from the natural world: heaven, earth, water, fire, thunder, wind, mountain, and lake. The hexagrams were named according to symbols mostly from the social world: "the Return," "Difficulty at the Beginning," "Before Completion," etc. All complexities aside, this creation sequence begins with the void and then progresses through seven stages of yin-yang polarization in which the physical process of creation is completed evolving from: (1) void, through (2) yin-yang (3) Four Images, (4) Eight Trigrams, and then (5) sixteen, and (6) thirty-two continuing subdivisions of yin and yang until (7) the sixty-four hexagrams are reached, which represent the completion of the yin-yang archetypal image preceding (8) the physical manifestation of the world (Dhiegh, 1973: 73).

YIN-YANG INTERPRETATION								
8 →	Materialization							
7 →								
6 →								
5 →								
4 →	Earth	Mountain	Water	Wind	Thunder	Fire	Lake	Heaven
3 →	Yin-in-Yin		Yang-in-Yin		Yin-in-Yang		Yang-in-Yang	
2 →	Yin				Yang			
1 →	Taiji							
0 →	Void							

In Chapter 7 of the *Zhuangzi* (350 to 222 BCE, one of the three major early Daoist texts including the *Daodejing* and the *Huainanzi*), a legendary version of these seven stages is recounted in the myth of Hundun. Hundun, whose name means "chaos," was a "cosmic-egg" type creature with no orifices in his body. He was also called the Emperor of the Central Region and, when visited by the two Emperor's of the North and South (symbolizing water and fire, see chart), treated them so generously that, to repay his kindness, they said (Yu, 1981: 481; Schipper, 1978: 360):

All men have seven openings so they can see, hear, eat, and breathe. But Hundun doesn't have any. Let's try to bore him some! Everyday they bored him another hole, and on the seventh day Hundun died.

In this story, the seven openings symbolize, not only the seven sensory orifices of the head and the opening of the unmanifest source to the external world, but also the seven polar stages of creation developing from the central void. It is interesting to note that this legend signifies that the birth of creation implies the death of, or disconnection from, the Source, a plight that, as we shall see, becomes fundamental to the Daoists.

The idea of creation emerging from a nondifferentiated void is also reflected in the *Daodejing* (Classic of the Source and Its Power), China's oldest Daoist text, generally believed to have been composed after Confucius sometime during the Warring States period (Feng, 1952: 170). Here the process of creation goes through four stages. The second chapter posits the origin of this sequence in Dao: "The origin of Heaven and Earth (*Dao*) is the mother of all things" (Wu, 1961: 3). In chapter 42, it describes the order of this sequence in symbolic detail (Wu, 1961: 60):

> Dao engenders the One, One engenders the Two,
> Two engenders the Three and the
> Three engenders the ten thousand things.[2]

In the *Daodejing*, Dao is equated with the void space of the *Yijing*; One is equated with Taiji; Two refers to yin and yang; Three is equated with the five levels of yin-yang interpenetration through the binary sequence (2, 4, 8, 16, 32, 64, etc.), which leads from the "Four Images" to the Eight Trigrams and sixty-four hexagrams; and Four is associated with the material world. The *Yijing* and *Daodejing* traditions are somewhat unified in the *Lu Shi Chun Qiu* (third century BCE), in which the term Taiji is replaced by *Taiyi* (the Supreme One), one of the divinities esteemed by the magical practitioners (*fangshi*) of this period (Robinet, 1990: 381-382).

Inherent in these early maps of creation was also the reverse path for returning to the Source. It was believed that, since the creation path led, in its extreme, to disharmony, disconnection from the Source, disease, and death, the "return" path led to renewal, healing, longevity, and, according to the ancients, immortality as well. The key to both of these maps is none other than the philosophical term taiji, the invisible gate between the unmanifest and the manifest. Ancient shamans travelled through this gate in their rituals to connect heaven and earth, and harmonize these two paths. This shamanistic activity is depicted etymologically in the word *ji* of taijiquan, which depicts a cosmic tree (*mu*) in this axis mundi function, through which the human supplicant (*ren*), or shaman, connects heaven and earth (*er*) through his words (*kou*, or chanting), and deeds (*you*, ritual actions), as signified by the moving of the arms (*you*) (Weiger, 1965). These shamanistic rituals were the earliest aspects of Chinese religious function, and their most important aspects (the ritual connection of heaven and earth, matter and spirit) were incorporated in highly significant ways in the historical development of later Chinese tradition of which Confucianism and Daoism were the most important. A thousand years later, all of these aspects came together in the formation of taijiquan.

	Stage	Yi Jing	Dao De Jing	Lu Shi Chun Qiu
THE CREATION SEQUENCE: PATH OF MANIFESTATION	0 →	Tai Xu (Great Void)	Dao	Taiyi (Great One)
	1 →	Taiji	Taiji	Taiji
	2 →	Yin and Yang	Yin and Yang	Yin and Yang
	3 →	Yin-Yang Interpenetration ("Four Images", Eight Trigrams: 16, 32, 64 Hexagrams)	Yin, Yang and Balance	Yin, Yang and Balance
	4 →	The Material World	The Material World	The Material World

The ideographic component of *ji*, from which *tian* and *di* (heaven and earth) are likewise derived, can symbolize a building's ridgepole from which the eaves spread out on either side. In Chinese temples, the most striking and unmistakable feature is the roof. "Instead of sitting simply on walls like the typical Western roof, it looks to be, as it structurally is, independent of the building itself; and therefore one has the impression that it is light and free despite its relatively massive proportions" (Thompson, 1989: 70). From this apparently immaterial ridgepole, the eaves extend, as if generating yin and yang as well as heaven and earth from the void, and ultimately sheltering the birth and death of the human activities carried out below.

Both Confucian and Daoist philosophers frequently cite that human activities as well as the creation of the world emerge from a common center to an increasingly complicated and diverse periphery. This emergence is frequently symbolized by the root, branches, stems, and flowers of a tree.

Creation and its activities are symbolized by the flowers, whereas the source of creation, the Great Void, Dao, or Taiyi, is symbolized by the root from which these flowers spring. Around 1130-1200 in the time of the legendary creation of taijiquan, Zhu Xi, the greatest neo-Confucian synthesizer, said: "Taiji is like a tree growing upward, it divides and becomes branches and stems... flowers and fruit... and continues until it produces seed" (Meyer, 1976: 32). The more one's consciousness becomes entangled in the flowers, the more one is cut off from the root. In as much as the expansion of the life force (*qi*) naturally tends toward its own dissipation as it reaches its periphery, all the great traditions of China have recognized in some form or another that for the life of the spirit to be maintained there must be some accompanying attention or even devotion to the periphery's corresponding center and source. These two directions give rise to the two paths of "creation" and "return." When the outgoing path of creation reaches its extreme in the devotion to material impulsess, such as greed, lust, pride, etc., there is a tendency to lose the connection to one's immaterial or spiritual source (*dao*) as well as the internal power or virtue (*de*) that it generates. Confucius called this materialistic path the path of the petty person or "small man" (*xiao ren*). In contrast, he called the more inner-directed path, even when it was connected horizontally through human relations, the path of the "great person" (*da ren*). The recognition and idealization of the "great person" gave rise to many other names, e.g., the sage (*junzi*) in Confucianism and the realized person (*zhen ren*) in Daoism. In effect, these were the saints of the ancient Chinese and were characterized, in essence, by their constant relation with *dao* and *de* through the connection of *dao* and *de* to taiji. The main difference was that in Confucianism, the sage applied the knowledge of these two paths horizontally in the social domain, while the realized person in Daoism applied them vertically to the natural and spiritual world.

Philosophy in Practice

The Daoist path of "return" is symbolically traversed by following the focus of one's intention in the reverse order of the creative path, i.e., from flower, to stem, to the small and then the large branches, and finally to the trunk and root. If we relate this metaphor, as well as the metaphors given in the *Yijing* and *Daodejing* creation maps cited above, to the most basic yin-yang aspects of taijiquan training, such as those found in the taijiquan sequence and described in the taiji classics, we will then be able to see how the return path of regeneration applies to taijiquan as a practical expression of these philosophies. To do this, we must substitute for the abstractions mentioned in the philosophical texts four of the most basic yin-yang aspects of taijiquan training. The taiji classics describe these four as (1) the in and out, opening and closing, movement of the breath including its connection to the joints; (2) movement itself with its corresponding yin stillness (*jing*) and yang action (*dong*); (3) the shifting of weight from substantial (*shi*) to insubstantial (*xu*, note that this term is the same word "empty" used for the Great Void itself); and (4) movement in the six directions (up/down, left/right, and forward/

backward) through a seventh neutral or pivot space (recall the seven stages of creation in the *Yijing* and the seven openings or movements of Hundun, the Emperor of Center). To incorporate these yin-yang principles into practice, we must begin with the basics of taijiquan standing postures, which are represented by Horse Stance, Bow Stance, Embrace the Pillar, and each of the thirty-seven postures of the taijiquan sequence on both the right and left sides. In the standing postures, external movement is reduced to the absolute minimum. In effect, there is no external yin-yang or outward motion except for the opening and closing of the breath and the joints. This simple opening and closing represents the taiji principle, prior to that is the nonbreathing, totally unmoving source that the philosophers call *wuji*, dao, or void, and following which is the sequence of the taijiquan form.

With this void space established, we begin to add the most basic movements (slow movements, of course) to our basic taijiquan sequence. In the Taiji Classics, it says that this movement is rooted at the feet, is generated from the legs, directed by the waist, and expressed in the fingers (Yang, 1987: 213). This movement begins by shifting our weight either from side to side in a medium to upright Horse Stance, or from front to back in Bow Stance. In this first aspect of shifting our weight, we have gone from point (taiji) to line (simple left, right, forward, or backward movement).

Now, from this simple shifting of weight from foot to foot, let us progress to the third stage, which is a circle. Focusing specifically on the origin of movement in the feet (done slowly), notice that the linear movement of weight, shifting from the substantial to the insubstantial foot, "grows" from a straight line to a curved line that "circles" under the feet in two directions when the movement shift to substantial has become complete. For example, when the weight on the right foot (substantial) shifts, the substantiality of that shifting should be perceived as the bottom of a circle traveling under the floor until it reaches the left foot, which then becomes substantial again. When the left foot starts to shift its substantiality back to the right, the top aspect of the circle moves up the left leg to the waist where it is then directed into the right leg, which then becomes substantial. This circle, then, continues throughout the exercise (right to left). At the same time, however, there is a circle rotating in the opposite direction (left to right). In other words, any time the substantial leg changes to insubstantial, there is a downward circle moving under the floor to the other leg and a corresponding upward circle moving up the substantial leg to the waist and down the other leg to the foot, where the two circles meet when the other leg becomes substantial. One has to keep the structural integrity of the body to experience these circles. This means that the feet, ankles, knees, and hips have to be in alignment. The knees should be held at the same height throughout the exercise. They should also be bent, but not poking out over the front or sides of the feet. This structural integrity allows the muscles to relax and the tendons and ligaments to be strengthened so that the body weight can be supported more by the skeletal system, which is designed specifically for this purpose.

The fourth stage of our progression now moves from circle to sphere by involving the expression of movement through the fingers (level 4 of the Taiji Classics). This fourth stage of progression from circle to sphere also corresponds to the fourth stage in the *Daodejing*, in which the "three begets the ten thousand things" (*wan wu*) or the created universe. At this stage, we add the motion of the arms and hands in, for example, any of the more complex thirty-seven postures of the Yang-style form. Picture any one of these postures being performed over and over again in a continuous sequence as they would be if they were linked together by doing them on both the right and left sides, one following the other. This sequence can be visualized more easily when the right and left versions of the postures follow one another in the sequence such as Brush Knee Twist Step, Repulse Monkey, Cloud Hands, etc. At this fourth stage, we have completed the "materialization" of our basic yin-yang principles through the taijiquan sequence as well as the creation path of materialization into the three-dimensional realm or sphere.

At this stage of movement, breath, as well as the shifting of weight from substantial to insubstantial, completes the top and bottom polarity of directions and becomes much more complex as the shift now includes the shoulders, arms, and fingers moving in relation to the waist, legs, and feet and encompasses the entire sphere of activity. Now, with the mind focused on these principles, imagine continuing through not only the rest of the thirty-seven postures but all of the movements of the taijiquan form. When one learns taijiquan in this manner, these yin-yang aspects are incorporated into the taijiquan sequence in the order following the creation path. Therefore, as in the *Yijing*, when the development of polarity reaches completion in the sixty-four hexagrams, all of the archetypal yin-yang aspects are now in place. The final materialization of the creative path here would be to apply this development either in a martial or healing situation or to use these principles in daily life. At this point of completion, the return path begins to establish these yin-yang aspects within the sequence on a deeper level in which each of these basic aspects, from the most basic to the most complex, is understood as the basis within the next

26

level. This process connects the expression of the entire sequence to its most basic foundation. The focused mind (*yi*) and body (*shen*) then discovers that the sequence is founded upon more and more basic principles.

IMAGE	STAGE	WEIGHT SHIFT	MOVEMENT IN CLASSICS	SUBSTANTIAL/ INSUBSTANTIAL		
No-thing	Wuji	None	None	None	← 0	**THREE-**
Point	Taiji	None	Breath-Joints	None	← 1	**DIMENSIONAL**
Line	Yin-Yang	In the feet	Rooted in Feet	Horizontal	← 2	**WEIGHT SHIFT**
Circle	Yin-Yang Interpenetration	To the waist	Directed by the waist	Horizontal & vertical	← 3	
Sphere	Manifestation	To the fingers	Flowers in the hands	Horizontal, vertical, & forward	← 4	

This process of discovery changes the performer into an observer deeply anchored in the still center of a heart now in resonance with the universe and at "one with the Dao." By practicing the choreographed and conscious sequence of taijiquan, our minds become aware, not so much of the peripheral phenomenal world, which is the realm of the "small person," but the perceiver of the whole of motion itself that lies within as our immortal spirit. We now have a map for mind and body that can act as a ritualized procedure with which we can, at any moment, return to where we started. By keeping the heart/mind on the polarities of yin-yang instead of the periphery of the external world, it is easier for the heart/mind to become aware of itself where, in the empty stillness of its center, the cosmic Source is found.

Alchemy, Rooting, and the Development of Jing

In their observations of heaven and earth's permutations, the ancient Chinese became aware of the polarity between transience and long life, the nurturance of which has been an overriding concern of the Chinese, especially the Daoists, since antiquity. There have been many phrases over the centuries that depict this fascination, including: *bao shen* (preservation of the visible individual); *nan lao* (to retard the advance of old age), which implies the retardation of senility; *que lao* (warding off old age); and *wu si* (deathlessness), all of which are "exemplified... in the common greeting and toast *wansui* 'May you live 10,000 years!'" (Knoblock, 1988: 114). The practices associated with these concepts, including alchemy (*jin dan*), a term first seen in Ge Hong's *Baopuzi* (265-419) (Barnes, 1936: 453), were the forefathers of both taijiquan and modern day qigong.

Chinese alchemy consists of both exoteric (*waidan*) and esoteric (*neidan*) aspects. Exoteric alchemy works with chemical substances in the laboratory to refine what is called the "elixir," which supposedly confers immortality upon those who take it. Esoteric alchemy, also called inner alchemy, works to refine the elixir within the human body through meditation. Both types of Chinese alchemy are fundamentally concerned with blending the polarities of matter and spirit so that each contains something from, and is transformed by, its opposite. This process not only spiritualizes, or vitalizes, matter, but also materializes, or concentrates, the spirit as well. Central to this idea is what the alchemists called the "three treasures": *jing, qi,* and *shen*, which are three different polar states of the life-force. *Jing* corresponds to earth, is the most material, and is stored in the kidneys and bones; *shen* corresponds to heaven, is the most spiritual, and is stored in the heart; and *qi* is in between, corresponding to man, and associated with the spleen and pancreas. Heaven, earth, and man were considered the cosmic triad in which heaven and earth come together, due to the man's participation, to form what is known as the "three powers" (*san cai*) (Bodde, 1991: 112).

The system of correspondence between the three treasures and the three powers also integrates with the system of the "five phases" (fire, soil, metal, water, and wood), which adds an additional dynamic to the three powers system in the same way that the equinoxes add a harmonizing dynamic to the more extreme polarities of the summer and winter solstices in the seasonal cycle. These three systems blend together so that the three treasures and three powers connect with the five phases and their more comprehensive associations, e.g., the primary organs of the body as well as specific emotions, psychic counterparts, and virtues. Thus, earth, representing matter, is associated with water, the kidneys, fear, will, and wisdom. In contrast, heaven, representing spirit, is associated with fire, the heart, elation or giddiness, spirit (*shen*, conscious awareness), and the ritualization of social relations and behavior. Between heaven and earth, the central harmonizing level of man is associated with soil, the spleen and pancreas, worry, intention, and trustworthiness.

Qualities of the Three Powers & Five Phases					
Three Powers	**Phase**	**Organ**	**Emotion**	**Psychic Counterpart**	**Virtue**
Heaven	Fire	Heart	Elation	Consciousness	Ritual
Man	Soil	Spleen	Worry	Intention	Trustworthiness
Earth	Water	Kidneys	Fear	Will	Wisdom

When the ancient Chinese examined the creation path (*sheng dao*) of the "small man," they realized that this path naturally reaches an extreme in which its very manifestation becomes worldly attachment. At this point, psychic loss as well as the loss of virtue prevail and the connection to the Source wears thin and breaks. In contrast, the return path (*fu dao*) of the "great man" embraces the void at the heart of Self, in which one's virtue and psyche are regenerated through a spontaneous process. The *Daodejing* describes the spirituality of the great man thusly (Wu, 1961: 9):

> Heaven lasts long, and Earth abides. What is the secret of their durability? Is it not because they do not live for themselves [i.e., worldly pursuits] that they can live so long? Therefore, the Sage (*sheng ren*) wants to remain behind, but he finds himself at the head of others; reckons himself out, but finds himself safe and secure. Is it not because he is selfless [i.e., in his non-pursuit of the world] that his Self is realized?

It seems as though the creative process itself, especially the separation of heaven and earth from the Great Void, automatically contains within it the seeds of its own dissolution. According to the *Huainanzi*, a Daoist text of 139 BCE (Girardot, 1983: 148):

> The pure yang (*qi*) drifted up and became heaven; and the heavy and turbid congealed downwards and became earth.... Heaven and earth unified their essence (*jing*) making yin and yang. Yin and yang blended and circulated their essence and produced the four seasons; and the four seasons in scattering their qi produced the ten thousand things.

In as much as yin and yang continue to blend with each other in the ongoing creation of life, the initial seed of separation continues to occur as well. After all, life and death are both aspects of yin and yang. This happens because the yin and yang, light and heavy, elements (meaning especially *jing* and *shen*) reach an extreme point at which they simultaneously recycle and interpenetrate to maintain the life form and separate from the body to maintain their connection with the Dao. After a period of time, the amount lost is more than that regained so that the spirit and body separate and death results.

The *Huainanzi* explains how the loss of spirit occurs (Roth, 1991: 643):

When perception comes in contact with external things, preferences are formed.... When preferences are formed, perception is enticed by externals, and one cannot return to the self [which is, then,] destroyed.

The progression of perception to preference ultimately leads to lust, greed, pride, fame, fortune, and pleasure, and becomes the ancient formula describing the path of the "small man." The ancients thought that the loss of *jing* (physical) and *shen* (spirit) through this progression was automatic unless there was some conscious intention to rectify it. The dissolution results in the water phase through the abuse of will so that *jing* leaks out below in the form of urinary incontinence, loss of sexual vitality, and senility. The dissolution results in fire when the spirit burns itself out above in direct proportion to one's indulgence, creating insomnia, heart disease, and loss of self through the ego's attachment to deluded thoughts, attitudes, and beliefs. Chapter 12 of the *Daodejing* admonishes (Wu, 1961: 15):

The five colours blind the eye.
The five tones deafen the ear.
The five flavors cloy the palate.
Racing and hunting madden the mind.
Rare goods tempt men to do wrong.
Therefore, the Sage takes care of the belly, not the eye.[4]
He prefers what is within to what is without.

And again in Chapter 52 (Wu, 1961: 73):

All-under-Heaven have a common beginning [the Source].
This Beginning is the Mother of the world.
Having known the Mother, we may proceed to know her children
[the flowers of creation], we should go back [return]
and hold on to the Mother [renew ourselves in the Source] . . .
Block all the passages!
Shut all the doors!
And to the end of your days you will not be worn-out.
[This refers to sense perception in pursuit of worldly desires.]
Open the passages! Multiply your activities!
And to the end of your days you will remain helpless
[The plight of the small man indeed].

The alchemists realized that if they could recycle more of their yin-yang elements, they could prolong life, perhaps even to the extreme state of "death-lessness" that they so ardently sought, and attain the Dao. Thus, they needed to insure that yin and yang continued their immortal interplay and that *jing* and *shen* did not leak away. Therefore, the exoteric alchemists came up with the idea of a closed container in which they would bury alchemical ingredients under ground so that they could not leak away and, therefore, be completely transformed in their interactions with one another (Needham, 1956: 4-6). The internal alchemists followed the same idea but used their intention (*yi*) to contain the alchemical process within the human body. We can also see this idea at work in Chinese herbalism in the most important kidney-strengthening formula, the "Six Flavor Rehmannia Decoction." This important formula uses only six herbs and focuses on the lead herb, Rehmannia, to create the physical and mental stillness so important for the kidneys and the water phase as well as for the practice of taijiquan. The ancient herbalists recognized that even the absolute stillness produced by Rehmannia could leak away so they included the astringent herb Cornus to contain Rehmannia's stillness (Kaptchuk, 1996).

We can also find this idea of containing the *jing* and *shen* in the Taiji Classics, in which the *yi* (psychic counterpart of the "power man," the phase soil, and the organs spleen and pancreas) takes on the function of container (Yang, 1987: 214):

> Up and down, forward and backward,
> left and right, it's all the same.
> All of this is done with the Yi....
> Elsewhere, the Classics build on this same idea (Yang, 1987: 228):
> [Throughout your] entire body,
> your mind [*yi*] is on the Spirit of Vitality
> [*jing shen*],[5] not on the [*qi*].

In taijiquan, it is easier to understand how intention (*yi*), as a closed container, can preserve and develop the *jing* and *shen* through the standing postures in which movement is reduced to its extreme slowness. Whereas the taijiquan sequence is characterized by continuous and repetitive motion through its thirty-seven basic postures, the standing postures are characterized by holding any one of these postures for an extended period of time (five to sixty minutes). What is most readily perceived while doing any of these postures is that they are difficult, if not impossible, to hold for more than a few minutes with muscular force alone. And yet a common, traditional way is for a beginner to hold these postures for up to an hour before any further work involving movement in the sequence is to be done. To achieve this, it is necessary to let go of muscular strength to go deeper in the body to the tendons, ligaments, and finally into the bones. In Chinese medicine, the bones are associated with the kidneys, the "earth power," and the water phase. The kidneys are the source of *jing*, which is stored, among other places, inside the bones in the marrow. The taiji classics say: "Condense (*lian*, literally draw together, *qian*, with the breath, *qian qi*) the qi into the marrow (*sui*) [or center of the bones]" (Yang, 1987: 234). The process of "condensing" *jing* into the bones in the standing postures is like storing more and more energy in a battery. At a certain point the *jing* and bones resonate with the earth's qi and one's deep root is established (Clay, 1996).

The containment of fire revolves around what in alchemy is called the fusion of *kan* and *li*. *Kan* and *li* are the names of the *Yijing* trigrams for water and fire and represent the third stage of manifestation, after the initial inter-penetration of yin and yang as heaven and earth, but prior to the creation of the hexagrams or even tangible things. In the body, *li* is in the top, heart region and *kan* is in the kidney region below. According to the *Yijing*, hexagram 64, "Before Completion" (Wilhelm, 1967: 249):

> When fire, which by nature flames upward, is above,
> and water, which flows downward, is below,
> their effects take opposite directions and remain unrelated.

The opposing directions of water and fire in this position is that of dissipation and separation. The archetypal stages of the creation path are characterized by yin-yang interpenetration, but once materialization has been achieved, the yin-yang principles gradually lose their attraction for each other and tend to go their separate ways, leaving one's existence "in a rather dubious state" (Wilhelm, 1967: 15). The purpose of the *kan* and *li* method is to return the opposing tendencies of water and fire to their original interpenetration. It does this by bringing the fire essence below that of water so that fire can steam the water essence into qi, which can then later become spirit, while bringing water to bear on fire so that the volatile spirit is subdued. Through this interpenetration, the opposing energies of water and fire, heaven and earth, are "returned" through the taiji gate to their central Source (e.g., *Dao*).

If the storage of *jing* in the bones is like the charging of a battery, then its transformation into spirit is like a generator. In the standing postures, at the same time that one sinks the *yi* and *qi* into the bones to concentrate the *jing*, one's conscious awareness is lowered automatically into its associated water realm. The result is that the heart/mind is stilled while the *jing* is increased. Stilling the mind and increasing the *jing* is also typically achieved through acupuncture and Chinese herbal medicine. As such, these practices are, along with these standing postures, an introduction into the alchemical *kan* and *li* procedures.

Placing the bones into the earth, if you will, to attract the *shen* is also a practice found in ancestor worship, especially in *feng shui* and its utilization in the ancient Chinese grave-siting practices. The ancients practiced both primary and secondary burials. The primary burial involves a process of one to two years, the purpose of which is to rot the flesh. After the flesh decays, the bones, which contain the ancestor's essence, are then dug up and placed in a container and reburied in a place where the bones are kept dry (Granet, 1930: 332). After they were placed in jars for secondary burial, the ancestors' bones were called "yellow gold," a name referring to alchemy and the transmutation of matter to spirit (Freedman, 1966: 29).[6] According to the *Zang Shu* or *Burial Book of Qiu Bu* (276-324 CE), the bones of the ancestors resonate with heaven and earth qi as well as with Dao itself. This resonance is then directed toward the living descendants, who thereby receive various benefits from both the ancestral spirits and their connection to the cosmic source (March, 1978: 29).

Chinese alchemy is derived from these much older practices of ancestor worship in which the interrelation between matter and spirit in relation to longevity and immortality practices first became important. To understand these interrelationships more completely in regard to the development of *shen* in taijiquan, we will now explore the connection of these ideas to sacrifice and ritual in the context of not only ancestor worship, but also the later development of Confucianism and Daoism, and finally the connection of each to the development and practice of taijiquan some thousand years later.

Sacrifice and Ritual in the Development of Shen

The practice of ancestor worship involves making an earthly and tangible offering, usually in the form of food and drink served in sacred vessels, to the spirits and ultimately their connection to *Dao* to secure *de* (i.e., their wisdom, blessing, and protection). Therefore, sacrificial offerings symbolize man in his mediating role between heaven and earth for the purpose of securing blessings.

Chinese ancestor worship attempts to contain the spirit(s) (bring them down) through the sacrifice of earthly, material things that alchemically represent the *jing* in the human body. Alchemy reiterates the earlier idea of external sacrifice found in Chinese ancestor worship but does so internally within the body and mind through the conversion of *jing* to spirit via the intermediary level of qi and intention (*yi*). Whereas in alchemy what "contains" the spirit(s) is *kan* and *li*, in Chinese ancestor worship it is what the ancient Chinese also called *li*, but signified with a different character meaning ritual. Both *li*, the trigram and the ritual, relate to fire in the five-phase system of correspondence that associates them both with the heart and spirit. Whereas the sound and association with the five phases of these two *li*'s is similar, there are also relevant differences. *Li*, the trigram, also carries the meaning of separation, leaving, and distance (Weiger, 1965: 617), which reflects the inherent scattering tendency of fire as discussed above; whereas ritual (*li*) connotes the containment of fire through sacrificial activity. In the Shang Dynasty, enormous attention was given to every conceivable detail of the royal sacrifice. These details were carefully orchestrated to correspond to seasonal and cosmic (astrological) events as well as to the particular ancestor or spirit to whom the sacrifice was directed. Thus, tremendous significance was given to the colors one wore, the kinds of nourishment one ate and drank, as well as to the specific actions and words that were used at specific times (recall the definition of the *ji* of "taiji" where the *wu* [shaman], to make life meaningful enough to bring the spirit[s] down, had to make his words and actions congruent).

Later, in the Zhou Dynasty (1122-255 BCE), Confucius made ritual into a virtue and, in so doing, made *li* (and *shen*) available to the common person by defining it as one of the three main aspects in the development of the "great man." For Confucius, it was not enough to simply perform the mechanics and technique of ritual, however perfectly that could be done. For ritual to truly qualify as Confucius' *li*, it had to be performed with great intention, but even more importantly, with the conscious awareness and feeling that characterize *shen*. Even though ritual contained aspects of mechanical actions, true ritual (*li*), required the presence of spirit. The intention behind Confucius' *li* was to create a symbolic learning situation, not unlike taijiquan, that would prepare his disciples for life in the everyday world by bringing something sacred to the mundane.

If you think about it, most of life is concerned with mechanical activity, and in the mundane world it is easy to become preoccupied with these affairs. You have to get up, get dressed, brush your teeth, cook your food, wash the pots, get to and from work, say hello, say good-bye, and on and on before any otherwise "meaningful" activity ever takes place. In his emphasis on *li*, Confucius was the first to realize the importance of a Zen-like "presence of mind" in the simple activities of daily life, e.g., chopping wood, carrying water, etc. Everyone has probably noticed that, in times of emotional stress (such as in great joy, grieving, anger, fear, worry, or even boredom), it is sometimes difficult to be fully present. Instead, the heart/mind (locus of the *shen*) drifts off toward an external image that may or may not correspond to what is actually happening. If one becomes traumatized into, or by, one of these emotions, one will then develop attitudes and beliefs about life that will make one prone to react to these attitudes and beliefs about life instead of responding directly to life itself. These false images spend the *jing* as the will chases illusory goals down wasteful paths that bear no return. According to Confucius, in times like these, *li* is what creates the container for spirit, keeping it linked to its surroundings, so that it can appropriately respond to the external world and thereby receive the blessings and protection (*de*) that Dao has to offer without losing itself either to the external world or one's imagination of it.

Xia Tao, President of the Hangshou Wuchu Association, practices a variety of taijiquan styles. He embodies the spiritual traditions of each style. Photography courtesy of D. Mainfort.

Taijiquan in Hangzhou, China. People gather along West Lake every morning before dawn to practice taiji and other exercises. The approach is holistic, combining traditions conducive for the mind, body, and spirit. Photograph by M. DeMarco.

Like alchemy, ritual contains spirit (*shen*) in the process of its transformation from *jing* and qi. If in the standing postures we build up a great quantity of *jing* and qi only to squander it away again in the transformation to spirit because there is nothing to contain it, then we not only lose the spirit, but the *jing* as well. This is a dangerous situation because the *jing* is the essence of material existence. If the heart's spirit is not trained to identify with its greater source in emptiness, external cravings will arise that lead one out to squander the *jing* in even greater amounts than before training because there simply is more power to waste. The irony is that, in doing so, what should become empty (the heart) now becomes full, whereas what should have been full (the kidney *jing*) becomes empty.

There is a fail-safe to this drawback built into the taijiquan sequence due to its embodiment of ritual. After all, taijiquan is a ritualized performance. Not only must one repeat the same sequence each time it is performed, but do so with intention and spirit. This means that one has to coordinate the opening and closing of the breath with the opening and closing of the joints, the three-dimensional movement from substantial to insubstantial and back again in the six directions throughout the progression of the thirty-seven postures and 108 or so movements. Performance on this level, as a starting point, certainly transcends mechanical action. The mind is unified with the body, the right (creative) and left (structured through ritual) sides of the brain are brought into balance, spirit and matter are coordinated, and heaven and earth are reunited through the return to the Source via the taiji (ridge) pole. In the Taiji Classics, it says that where the heart/mind goes the qi will follow (Weiger, 1965: 617).

(Throughout your) entire body, your mind [yi]
is on the Spirit of Vitality [jing shen], not on the [qi].
[If concentrated] on the [qi], then stagnation.
A person who concentrates on [qi] has no li [strength];
a person who cultivates [qi] [develops] pure hardness [power].

"That which goes against the Way will come to an early end."
– Laozi, Ch. 55

In Yunnan province,, a man on the streets of Kunming city
proudly displays his long white beard. A long beard,
like long noodles, is a symbol of longevity.
Photograph by M. DeMarco.

This means that when one keeps the intention focused on the *jing shen* (an aspect of spirit) instead of the qi, or any other phenomena that may occur in practice, what develops is spirit.

At this point, taijiquan practice turns into play as the spontaneous movement of qi expressing itself naturally from its source is experienced. The taiji classics speak thusly of this spontaneity (Yang, 1987: 232):

> The true nature of the Heart [xin xing] as well as the Intention [yi] should be calm [jing], and then spontaneity [zuran] will miraculously [ling] appear from nowhere [wu].[7]

This calmness (jing), or quiescence, is a Daoist technical term used to refer to the root state preceding birth. According to the Zhuangzi (Rickett, 1960: 227),

> From emptiness comes quiescence; from quiescence comes movement; and from movement comes attainment. From quiescence comes non-activity [wuwei, stillness] and when [the ruler] [Heart] is non-active, those in charge of affairs may assume their responsibilities.

There are several paradoxes at play here through which apparently simple things turn to their opposite. Turning away from the outward directed path of life to the path of return creates not death, but an everlasting spiritual life. Turning away from the fire-like, externally directed movement of spirit to embrace the most earthly energy of jing, provides the foundation and perpetuation of spirit. Placing one's spirit in a "container" through the ritualization of the taijiquan sequence results in the deepest and most comprehensive level of spontaneity revered by the ancient masters and saints. Perhaps these paradoxes are symbolized in the legendary creation of taijiquan through the battle between the bird and the snake. After all, these are, in fact, the traditional Chinese symbols of the water and fire interaction discussed above.

Chinese Romanization Chart 1

Pinyin	Wade-Giles	Chinese
bagua	pa¹ kua⁴	八卦
bao shen	pao³ shen¹	保身
can	ts'an¹	參
da ren	ta⁴ jen²	大人
dantian	tan¹ t'ien¹	丹田
dao	tao⁴	道
de	te²	德
di huang	ti⁴ huang²	地黃
dong	tung⁴	動
er	erh⁴	二
feng shui	feng¹ shui³	風水
fu	fu⁴	復
fu	fu⁴	腹
fu dao	fu⁴ tao⁴	復道
gen	ken¹	根
gua	kua⁴	卦
huang jin	huang² chin¹	黃金
hundun	hun⁴ tun⁴	混沌
ji	chi²	極
jin dan	chin¹ tan¹	金丹
jing shen	ching¹ shen²	精神
jing	ching¹	精
jing	ching⁴	靜
junzi	chün¹ tzu³	君子
kou	k'ou³	口
li	li³	禮
li	li²	離
lian	lien⁴	斂
ling	ling²	靈
mu	mu⁴	木
nan lao	nan² lao³	難老
nei dan	nei⁴ tan¹	內丹
qi	ch'i⁴	氣
qian	ch'ien	欠
qian	ch'ien	僉
quan	ch'üan²	拳
que lao	ch'üeh⁴ lao³	卻老

Chinese Romanization Chart 2

Pinyin	Wade-Giles	Chinese
ren	jen^2	人
san cai	san^1 ts'ai^2	三才
shen	shen^2	神
sheng ren	sheng^1 jen^2	聖人
sheng dao	sheng^1 tao^4	生道
shi	shih^2	實
shou	shou^3	手
sui	sui^3	髓
taijiquan	t'ai^4 chi^2 ch'üan^2	太極拳
tai ji	t'ai^4 chi^2	太極
tai xu	t'ai^4 hsü^1	太虛
tian di	t'ien^1 ti^4	天地
tu	t'u^3	土
wai dan	wai^4 tan^1	外丹
wan sui	wan^4 sui^4	萬歲
wan wu	wan^4 wu^4	萬物
wu	wu^1	巫
wu	wu^2	無
wu ji	wu^2 chi^2	無極
wu si	wu^2 ssu^3	無死
wu wei	wu^2 wei^2	無為
xiang	hsiang^4	象
xiao ren	hsiao^3 jen^2	小人
xin	hsin^4	信
xin xing	hsin^1 hsing^4	心性
xu	hsu^1	虛
yang sheng	yang^3 sheng^1	養生
yi	i^2	儀
yi	i^4	意
you	yu	又
yuan	yüan^2	元
zhang sheng	chang^3 sheng^1	長生
zhen ren	chen^1 jen^2	真人
zhi	chih^4	志
zhi	chih^4	智
zhu	chu^3	主
ziran	tzu^4 jan^2	自然

Notes

[1] This progression follows what is called the binary sequence, in which each level multiplies itself by two, i.e., 1, 2, 4, 8, 16, 32, etc.

[2] Translation is mine.

[3] The wood and metal phases fit here in their association with man but are, however, irrelevant to this discussion.

[4] The Chinese word "belly" (*fu*) rhymes with "return" (*fu*), and is also etymologically similar. The belly, or *dantian* (literally "elixir field"), is the locus classicus of Daoist meditation (Weiger, 1965).

[5] I prefer translating the term *jing shen* as "concentrated awareness."

[6] Alchemy was often called the art of the "yellow and white," with yellow referring to gold and white to silver. Gold and silver were two of the main symbols for yang and yin respectively.

[7] Translation is mine.

Bibliography

Barnes, W. (October 1936). Diagrams of Chinese chemical apparatus. *Journal of Chemical Education*, 453.

Bodde, D. (1991). *Chinese thought, society, and science: The intellectual and social background of science and technology in pre-modern China*. Honolulu: University of Hawaii Press.

Clay, A. (August 6, 1996). Personal interview.

Dhiegh, K. A. (1973). *The eleventh wing: An exposition of the dynamics of the i ching for now*. New York: Dell Publishing Company.

Feng, Y. L. (1952). *A history of Chinese philosophy, vol. 1*. (D. Bodde, Trans.). Princeton: Princeton University Press.

Freedman, M. (1966). *Chinese lineage and society*. London: University of London, The Athlone Press.

Girardot, N. (1983). *Myth and meaning in early Taoism: The theme of chaos (hun-tun)*. Berkeley: University of California Press.

Granet, M. (1930). *Chinese civilization*. (K. Innes and M. Brailsford, Trans.). London: Kegan Paul, Trench, Tribner and Co. Ltd.

Kaptchuk, T. (1996). A course in Chinese herbalism. Unpublished course notes. Arlington, VA.

Needham, J. (1956). *Science and civilization in China, Vol. 5*. Cambridge: Cambridge University Press.

Knoblock, J. (1988). *Xunzi: A translation and study of the complete works, vol. 1, books 1-6*. Stanford: Stanford University Press.

March, A. (1978). The winds, the waters and the living qi. *Parabola* 3/1: 29.

Meyer, J. (1976). *Peking as a sacred city.* Taipei: Oriental Culture Service.

Rickett, W. (1960). An early Chinese calendar chart: Kuan-tzu, Book III, Chapter 8. *T'oung Pao Archives,* 48: 227.

Robinet, I. (1990). The place and meaning of the notion of taiji in Taoist sources prior to the Ming dynasty. *History of Religions,* 29/4: 381-382.

Roth, H. (1991). Psychology and self-cultivation in early Taoist thought. *Harvard Journal of Asiatic Studies,* 51: 643.

Schipper, K. (1978). *The Taoist body. History of Religions,* 17: 360.

Sung, Z. (1935). The text of the Yi King (and its appendixes). Shanghai: The China Modern Education Company.

Thompson, L. (1989). *Chinese religion: An introduction.* Belmont, CA: Wadsworth Publishing Company.

Weiger, L. (1965). *Chinese characters: Their origin, etymology, history, classification and significance.* New York: Paragon.

Wilhelm, R. (1962). *The secret of the golden flower: A Chinese book of life.* New York: Harcourt, Brace & World, Inc.

Wilhelm, R. (1967). *I ching or book of changes.* (C. Baynes, Trans.). New York: Bollingen Foundation.

Wu, J., (Trans.). (1961). *Lao Tzu: Tao te ching.* New York: St. John's University Press.

Yang, J. (1987). *Advanced Yang style tai chi chuan, vol. 1: Tai chi theory and tai chi jing.* Jamaica Plain, NY: YMAA Publications.

Yu, D. (1981). The creation myth and its symbolism in classical Taoism. *Philosophy East and West,* 31: 481.

· 3 ·

Taijiquan as an Experiential Way for Discovering Daoism

by Michael A. DeMarco, M.A.

As the alleged founder of Daoism, Laozi retired from
his worldly occupation and departed westward on an ox.
Legends give many fanciful embellishments to the story.
However, the artistic renderingsby Oscar Ratti
accompanying this chapter invite the reader to create
a personal interpretation. All illustrations courtesy of
© 1997 Futuro Designs & Publications.

Introduction

If someone without any previous exposure to Daoist philosophy began
to study taijiquan, what would he or she learn regarding taiji's fundamental
principles? And how closely would the resulting philosophical insights concur
with Daoist tenets?—The following presents a way of directly discovering
taiji boxing's philosophical principles through experiential involvement in
the art itself. There certainly is no real need for delineating historical roots
with footnotes here, but only rooting our feet in taiji.[1]

We will first look at the learning process involved from a student's viewpoint. The philosophical insights gained through this practice will be indicated as they arise during this learning process. A summary of these philosophical principles can then be compared to those found in the Daoist tradition.

Learning Taijiquan's Solo Form

Regardless of the taiji style being taught, a new student begins by learning a solo routine that contains a series of movements which, depending on its length and tempo, takes five to forty minutes to perform. While learning the solo routine, the student's main objective is to become aware of how the body moves. During this initial stage, martial applications are usually not taught so that the student may focus on himself without distraction.

The instructor simply demonstrates a movement and lets the student repeat it. Consecutive movements are shown one-by-one according to the student's readiness until the complete series of movements is memorized. The learning process here involves little or no discussion between teacher and student. A student learns by copying the master's techniques and repeating them thousands of times. The understanding of how the techniques are executed is gained largely through intuition and awareness resulting from hours of devoted practice. What is learned through this practice gives an evolving definition of "taijiquan," a definition which changes with time according to one's ever-deepening insights into the art. However, practice of the solo form should demonstrate all the fundamental principles for which taijiquan is noted.

In order to simplify a presentation on taijiquan practice, the following material focuses on the Yang-style, but similarities would be found in other branches as well. Traditional Yang taiji is composed of over one hundred movements strung together in three sections. From the beginning posture comes the first step, then the second step, and the form continues in a flowing sequence of movements which closes with a posture that is exactly like the beginning posture. The compositional structure of the sequence itself is very similar to a symphony with its own melodic flow of changing passages held together by repetitive bars to form an overall unity. Even though a symphony may contain a highly complex inner structure, its unity can be recognized as a singular "masterpiece."

After many months, regular practice brings a familiarity with the solo form and the practitioner becomes more and more comfortable with the routine.

The movements seemingly begin to flow of their own accord, releasing mental and physical stress found in students at the beginning level. By the time the complete routine is learned, the student can enter the door of discovery that allows an experiential sensing of taiji's philosophical core.[2]

Principles Derived from the Solo Routine Practice

Upon first observing the traditional Yang routine, most new students are apprehensive of the number and complexity of movements. They ask, "How is it possible to remember all those movements in sequence?" They later realize that the movements are not as difficult to learn as they first appeared, especially when learning only one movement at a time. Within the routine itself, many movements are repeated in whole or in part.

By the time the student has completed learning the routine, he has a distinct sense for the three sections. Furthermore, he sees individual movements as parts of sequences. Where there was once "brush knee, twist-step left, twist-step right, twist-step left," there is now simply the "brush knee sequence." The same, for example, can be said for "the three kicks," "four corners," or "cloud hands." As the practitioner gains greater familiarity with the routine, he sees such sequences as forming parts of even longer sequences.

Analyzing the individual taiji movements, we find that each movement is brought about by a simple change in body posture, with one simple change leading to other changes. Shifting of body weight in the legs and feet is easily sensed, particularly in taiji routines which are practiced in a very slow manner. As one leg becomes "full" with weight, the other is "emptied" and capable of moving in any chosen direction. The body's trunk remains in balance over the legs as the hands follow the waist in deflecting left or right; striking, pressing, or pushing forward; rolling-back or "repulsing monkey." These horizontal movements are coupled with vertical movements as well. This is particularly noticeable in "snake creeps downward" and "rooster stands on one leg," since these are extremes of low and high following one another. But vertical movement should be equally sensed throughout the routine, commencing with "taiji beginning."

Whether we look at the complex composition of the complete Yang routine or the individual movements which form it, there develops an underlying sense of flow that unites all the movements. The taiji solo routine is often compared to the slow, steady flow of a long river. It is this flow which provides the continuity and wholeness of the routine. All of the movement from "beginning" to "conclusion" is performed in smooth even tempo with no clear demarcation to signify where one technique begins or ends.

Reflecting on the learning process involved in taiji, the student becomes aware that taiji's complexity is simplified by grouping certain movements into sequences. In turn, these small sequences form part of larger sequences, often simply referred to as the traditional "three sections" for convenience. However, all taiji movements find their source in the most basic principle of change. At an advanced level, the practitioner finds himself changing effortlessly from one movement to another. An observer cannot tell where one technique ends and the next begins. The sequence of movements connects as a single thread and the exercise feels like a unified routine.

Taiji as practiced by an accomplished master looks easy to do, but the necessary skills take years to hone. For the beginner, practice is characterized by tenseness, staccato movements, and off-balanced postures. How do these evolve into taiji characterized by balance, smoothness, and relaxed grace? Taiji body mechanics can be summed up in one word: naturalness.

The slow-motion Yang-style routine magnifies the awareness of each movement, which, in turn, allows the practitioner to feel what makes his movements cumbersome and offers direction for making appropriate corrections within each movement. Consciously and subconsciously, the movements can be transformed from a rustic set of physical exercises into a true martial art routine.

Solo Routine Principles and Daoist Tenents

The preceding section outlines a typical mode of learning Yang-style taiji and presents some of the common psychological insights associated with the practice. These insights are gained through the practice itself, but what of the Daoist flavor is expressed, if any? Any similarities or differences between the two we can find by comparing the contents of the preceding section with principles long held as the most fundamental to Daoism.

Ten Thousand Things in the Way

The Chinese have traditionally viewed the world as composed of "ten thousand things." Things, infinitely numerous in shapes and sizes, dazzle our senses with an ever-changing kaleidoscope of colors, sounds, aromas, tastes and textures. From birth, we are forced to find our place within this ever-turning world. The philosophy we develop can provide the wisdom and skills that determine how successful we will be. It is our means for survival.

During the formation of early Chinese culture, it was recognized that, in order to solve any complex problem, the "ten thousand things" surrounding the matter must first be simplified. What is the most important aspect of the problem? What roles do other factors play which are really significant? Through such questioning the Chinese were actually developing a highly sophisticated mode of logic and reasoning. They found it useful to categorize the "ten thousand things" to better adapt to their environment.

A parallel can be found in taijiquan practice, in which the student is initially confused by the "ten thousand" movements. Here the student is challenged to find a way to properly master the complexity of all the movements. A step along this path involves the discovery of categories by which the taiji movements can be better understood and performed.

The Ways and Means of Five Forces (wuxing)

Stopping to contemplate the world, insightful Chinese viewed the "ten thousand things" that appeared between Heaven and Earth. They looked closely in every direction. As a person peers outward, he realizes that he himself forms the center of his existence, the center of the universe. Perhaps this orientation between man and his universe led the Chinese to the idea of *wuxing*. Likewise, a taiji practitioner is the ever-present center of the moving art form of taiji.

An analysis of the characters *wu* and *xing* helps us clarify the general meaning usually given to the compound term as Five Forces. *Wu* simply stands for the number five. In ancient times, it was written like an "X," where four lines indicated the directions from a common central focus. Later, a line was placed above and another below the "X," symbolic of Heaven and Earth. This is similar to man's position on Earth. Only from his own viewpoint can he look out into all directions under Heaven.

Xing carries with it such meanings as to go, operate, conduct or set into motion. Combined with *wu*, we have five active forces, or movers. They represent five basic phases through which matter continuously transforms itself. As a concept, *wuxing* stands for abstract forces, five movers which keep the "ten thousand things" in operation.

Besides being associated with the five spatial directions (north, south, east, west, and center), the *wuxing* concept was conveniently and suitably applied to other aspects of nature. A partial list indicates its significance as a comprehensive tool for understanding the "ten thousand things." In particular, it often was associated with the seasons, animals, weather, bodily organs, numbers, musical notes, colors and even flavors.

How do the Five Forces work? According to Daoist philosophy, they work quite easily! Just as one season naturally follows another, any one phase is connected to the next. Plus, all phases are interrelated in some way, each having its own characteristics and influences. In short, each plays its part in an overall process of construction and destruction that keeps the "ten thousand things" in movement. Due to cause and effect, they flow in cycles, passing from one phase to the next until completing a circuit. By an intimate understanding of the laws involved in such changes, man can better adapt himself to the continual changes in the world.

The Five Forces theory became so important that an independent school of philosophy arose under its name during the fourth and third centuries BCE. In the third century BCE, a strategist named Zou Yan made it a regular feature of political theory. Kingdoms, under the influence of a given *wuxing* phase, rose and fell in predictable order much like earth produces wood, which in turn is destroyed by fire.

The theory of Five Forces was applied to all fields of study, including astronomy, divination, medicine, agriculture, politics, art, and religion. It served as a valuable schematic upon which subjects could be analyzed and understood within their specialized sphere of changing relationships. Thus, within their changes, an underlying order and permanence could still be found.

China's ancient philosophers were seeking the wisest way to obtain the insight and skills necessary to master life. Although the *wuxing* theory proved very practical, its application was actually still so complex that only the most gifted of sages could successfully employ it to advantage. It is too easy to become entangled by five everchanging variables. Laozi was clearly aware of this, writing:

The five colors cause one's eyes to go blind.... The five flavors confuse one's palate. The five tones cause one's ears to go deaf. Therefore, in the government of the Sages: He is for the belly and not for the eyes. Thus he rejects that and takes this.

– Henricks, 1989: 64 (Ch. 12)

The *wuxing* were understood to be the simplified basis of the "ten thousand things." In order to be more workable, would it be possible to simplify further? Chinese sages did just that—they categorized the world into two: yin and yang. In so doing, the *wuxing* became easier to understand and, therefore, so did the "ten thousand things."

In a similar manner, the taiji practitioner eventually finds order within the complexity of movements comprising the routine. Some practitioners become so infatuated with individual techniques that they miss the overall importance of the system! They do not heed Laozi's advice and get lost in the "ten thousand" movements. Others focus on the complete routine. After the routine is categorized into sections and sequences become familiar, the routine is performed with less difficulty. From the starting movement the practitioner feels as if he is moving through sections of the routine rather than many individual movements, until the end which completes the cycle.

The Bi-Ways of Yin and Yang

We walk a road with two feet, view the world through only two eyes. In the fourth century BCE, at roughly the same time the *wuxing* theory developed, the Chinese also formulated a polar view of the world with the theory of yin-yang. By the Han Dynasty (202 BCE-220 CE), this Yin-Yang School absorbed that of *wuxing*. Together they offered a comprehensive system useful not only for analysis, but also in the control and manipulation of all areas to which they were applied.

There are earthy roots to the yin-yang theory. It is believed that the ancient characters derived in part as symbolic images of the daily fluctuation between day and night, or more precisely, light and dark. The yang character shows the sun on the horizon, radiating its brilliance down on the earth. Yin is composed of *jin*, meaning "now" and *yun* meaning "cloudy." As a result, yin became associated with cloud-like characteristics, including cold, night, shade, dark, and water. Similarly, yang came to imply a varied list of sun-like attributes, such as hot, day, clear, bright, and fiery. The written characters have changed over the centuries into their simplified modern versions. However, the implications do remain the same as those of the original characters. Oddly enough, no written character can fully express the meaning with which yin-yang became associated.

Since the symbolism of language failed to convey the meaning of yinyang, a more appropriate symbol was required. Of all of the cosmological diagrams invented in China, the taiji symbol is no doubt the most famous. It also remains the most useful symbol for expressing the yin-yang theory. The characters for taiji should first be analyzed before discussing the symbol itself.

When the characters for *taiji* are broken down, the individual character *tai* we find refers to something "very big" or "extreme." It resembles a stick figure who is stretching his limbs out to their limits in four directions. *Ji* is more complicated. It also has a significance of "extreme," but more importantly a "pole," the extreme of any axis. In ancient times, *ji* was a common word for "ridgepole" upon which the structure of a house would rest. With reference to cosmology, taiji is the "Supreme Ultimate Principle," the cosmological ridgepole which supports the whole universe.

In philosophical terms, the taiji is the Absolute. It is the most basic principle upon which *wuxing* and the "ten thousand things" rest. An Absolute is so limitless and pervasive that it does not have any visible signs to be perceived. For this reason, yin-yang became its first visible attributes.

The symbol for the taiji, or Supreme Ultimate, is the intertwining of yin and yang. The parts are not static, but are constantly in movement, varying their relationship in fluctuating percentages or even transforming one into the other. Through the varied interactions of yin-yang, the universe is kept in motion. No aspect of creation exists without their signature. Laozi wrote:

> The ten thousand things carry yin on their backs and wrap their arms
> around yang. Through the blending of qi (their energies) they arrive
> at a state of harmony.
>
> — Henricks, 1989: 11 (Ch. 42)

The yin-yang interplay is the foundation of taiji's boxing routine. It is the impetus of the flowing movements. Throughout the taiji routine, practitioners experience the fluctuating pulse of yin and yang. How this categorization functions in taiji is shown through the following examples:

50

YIN		YANG
closed		open
inward		outward
hidden		shown
slow		fast
soft		hard
mind		body
sinking		rising
down		up
low		high
passive		active
back		front
inside		outside
light		heavy
north		south
empty		full
defensive		offensive
receiving		giving
curved		straight
round		square
pull		push
retreat		advance

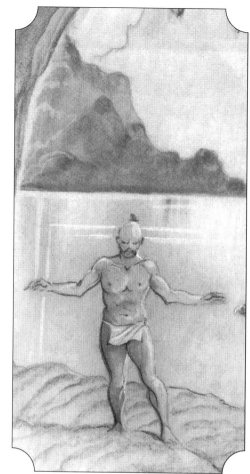

In Daoism, *wuxing* and yin-yang serve to categorize the "ten thousand things." This helps one to understand the universe in its varied aspects. *Wuxing* and yin-yang also demonstrate how the universe operates. The experience of taiji boxing likewise illustrates the flow of movement through positional phases and fluctuations between yin and yang. On an even more subtle level, movement is brought about from stillness. Stillness is found in the Dao.

Dao: The High-Way of Daoism

The *Daodejing* states:

> There was something formed out of chaos,
> that was born before Heaven and Earth.
> Quiet and still! Pure and deep!
> It stands on its own and doesn't change.
> It can be regarded as the mother
> of Heaven and Earth. I do not know
> its name: I style it "the Way."
>
> — Henricks, 1989: 77 (Ch. 25)

Carl Jung said that the "value of Dao lies in its power to reconcile opposites on a higher level of consciousness" (Chang, 1970: 3). We find this in the highest levels of taijiquan practice.

It is made known when the practitioner transcends the complexity of the "ten thousand" movements, transcends the arbitrary groupings of sequential techniques, transcends even the mind-body duality. This is a mystic state which does not limit itself to taiji boxing.

A dominant thought existing in Laozi's time is found in the *Book of Odes*: "Heaven in producing mankind annexed its laws to every faculty and relationship. Man possessed of this nature should strive to develop his endowment to perfection." A "Heavenly Identity," or Dao-realization, comes to one through polishing the mirror-like mind, cleansing away its mundane dust. Zhuangzi called this a process of "purifying the mind." Laozi further advised one to rid himself of desires in order to observe the Dao's secrets (Lau, 1963: 57).

Dao realization is of great importance because whoever attains this state takes on all the attributes of the eternal Dao. Why this is important in taijiquan and other martial arts can be discerned from a quote from the *Daodejing*, Ch. 16: "If you're one with the Dao, to the end of your days you'll suffer no harm" (Henricks, 1989: 68).

The Dao is described in Chinese literature as being complete and whole. As such, it is the abode of stillness and tranquility. It is the "mother of the ten thousand things." "The Way [Dao] gives birth to them, nourishes them, matures them, completes them, rests them, rears them, supports them, and protects them" (Henricks, 1989: 20).

Daoism	Taijiquan
"10,000 things"	Over one hundred movements in the Yang Taiji routine.
Five Elements	Three sections into which the Yang Taiji routine is divided.
Yin-Yang	Duality inherent in each taiji movement.
Dao	The oneness of the unified taiji routine.
De	The virtue/power expressed in taiji movements.

Conclusion

A student of taiji boxing passes through various psychological stages in experiencing the complexity of the routine. At first a mysterious hodge-podge of techniques, the numerous movements within the routine become easier to understand and perform as regular practice brings a familiarity with the set. The *wuxing* and yin-yang concepts help one understand the underlying process of change within the routine. We also learn the inherent relationship that exists within the unity of all body parts as utilized in the movements.

However, at the highest level of practice the completeness and wholeness of the taiji routine find a parallel in the oneness of Dao. When the dualism of mind and body are transcended, the taiji routine seems to flow of its own accord. It is as spontaneously natural as a flowing river. This is taiji in the state of "non-doing" (*wuwei*). A solo performance in this state is characterized by tranquility and freedom from thought, which for the martial artist has other implications as well. It makes the power (*de*) of Dao available, for in self-defense it is necessary to move spontaneously with the accuracy and strength possible only through the complete unification of human thought and movement.

What we have analyzed in this chapter is the discovery of Daoist principles in the taijiquan routine. Here, the inner workings of the individual are found, presenting the physical and mental operations as they are seen in the solo routine. There are also other taiji practices, such as push-hands and a paired form. These practices seek to let the individual discover his relationship with others.

For the Daoist, this may be the ultimate reason why the name "taiji" was chosen for this boxing style.

Notes

1 An earlier version of this chapter was presented at the 73rd annual meeting of the Central States Anthropological Society on March 21-24, 1996, in Covington, KY. Laozi writes: "Throw away knowledge, and the people will benefit a hundredfold" (Henricks, 1989: 71). In Daoist fashion, I have tried to minimize the academic documentation in this present version in order to focus on actual experience.

2 There is a strong tradition among Western scholars to categorize Daoism according to its use in Chinese society, with philosophical and religious Daoism forming the two major categories. Again, I have chose to ignore the standard approach in favor of the Daoist unitary vision. This holds true even with the philosophical concepts mentioned in this chapter, since they may fall under other philosophical schools of thought as well, e.g., Confucianism.

Acknowledgements

Appreciation goes to Barbara Davis, Michael Davis, and Douglas Wile for reading and making suggestions for improving this chapter. As I did not heed all of these suggestions, I will bear the burden for any faults found in the final draft. An appreciative salute is given to Oscar Ratti for his appropriate artwork. He brings to life the essence of the Chinese proverb: "What is accomplished in the mind, is made known by the hand."

Bibliography

Blofeld, J. (1978). *Taoism: The road to immortality*. Boulder, CO: Shambhala Publications, Inc.

Bodde, D. (1978). *Harmony and conflict in Chinese philosophy. Studies in Chinese Thought*. (A. Wright, Ed.). Chicago: University of Chicago Press, 19-80.

Breslow, A. (1995). *Beyond the closed door: Chinese culture and the creation of t'ai chi ch'uan*. Jerusalem: Almond Blossom Press.

Chang, C. (1970). *Creativity and taoism*. New York: Harper and Row Publishers, Inc.

Chen, Y. (n.d.). *T'ai-chi ch'uan: Its effects and practical applications*. Hong Kong: n.p.

DeMarco, M. (1983). The mirror-like mind of taoism and its implications for the individual and society. Ann Arbor, MI: University Microfilms International. Master's thesis for Seton Hall University, 1981.

Finazzo, G. (1968). *The notion of tao in the Lao Tzu and the Chuang Tzu*. Taipei: Mei Ya Publications.

Fung, Y. (1966). *A short history of Chinese philosophy*. (D. Bodde, Ed.). New York: The Free Press.

Henricks, R. (Trans.) (1989). *Lao-Tzu te-tao ching*. New York: Ballantine Books.

Huang, A. (1993). *Complete tai-chi: The definitive guide to physical and emotional self-improvement*. Rutland, VT: Charles E. Tuttle Co.

Jou, T. (1981). *The tao of tai-chi chuan: Way to rejuvenation*. Warwick, NY: Tai Chi Foundation.

Kaltenmark, M. (1969). *Lao Tzu and taoism*. (R. Greaves, Trans.). Stanford, CA: Stanford University Press.

Kuo, L. (1994). *The t'ai chi boxing chronical*. (Guttmann, Trans.). Berkeley, CA: North Atlantic Books.

Lau, D. (Trans.). (1963). *Lao Tzu tao te ching*. Baltimore, MD: Penguin

Books Inc.

Maspero, H. (1981). *Taoism and Chinese religion.* (F. Kierman, Trans.). Amherst, MA: The University of Massachusetts Press.

Needham, J. (1956). *Science and civilization in China. Vols. I and II.* Cambridge: Cambridge University Press.

Waley, A. (Trans.). (1962). *The way and its power: A study of the tao te ching and its place in Chinese thought.* New York: Grove Press, Inc.

Watts, A. (1975). *Tao: The watercourse way.* New York: Pantheon Books, Inc.

Welch, H. (1965). *Taoism: The parting of the way.* Boston, MA: Beacon Press.

Welch, H., and Seidel, A. (Eds.). (1979). *Facets of taoism.* New Haven: Yale University Press.

Wile, D. (1996). *Lost t'ai-chi classics from the late ch'ing dynasty.* Albany, NY: State University of New York Press.

Wong, K. (1996). *The complete book of tai chi chuan: A comprehensive guide to the principles and practice.* Rockport, MA: Element Books, Inc.

· 4 ·

Immortality in Chinese Thought and Its Influence on Taijiquan & Qigong
by Arieh Lev Breslow, M.A.

The Nine Dragon Pond within Hua Qing (Glorious Purity) Hot Springs. The springs were first used for medicinal purposes and became the site of a Daoist monastery in 936. Located just outside of Xi'an city, the area served as a resort for emperors and royalty for over a thousand years. Photographs by M. DeMarco.

Immortality is an age-old dream of human beings. Ancient and modern people, East and West, have confronted the same dilemma: the absurdity of death and the loss of personal ego. For most of us, it is an unsettling thought that we will grow old, become infirm, and eventually die. Western traditions have dealt with death in many ways. Judaic-Christian teachings promise the resurrection of the dead in the Messianic age. Against the specter of death, modern science has marshaled the technologies of cloning and cryogenics. In both the East and the West, there are an infinite number of products on the market that promise youth and vitality.

Chinese philosophers have always concerned themselves with immortality. Ge Hong and the religious Daoists believed that they could manufacture a pill that would keep them forever young and transform themselves into immortals. Through meditation and special exercises like qigong and more recently taijiquan, Daoists wanted to purify their coarse bodies into subtle spirit and merge with the infinite and eternal *Dao* (Way). This chapter will examine the origins of immortality in Chinese thought and introduce its influence on qigong and taijiquan.

Religion and Immortality in China

Throughout the centuries, religious attitudes and feelings have played a powerful role in Chinese society. In addition to Confucianism, Daoism, and Buddhism, other native philosophies and superstitions existed. Various powerful gods—each with his or her own turf—required prayers and offerings as payment to safeguard family and home. In his classic study on Chinese religion, C. K. Yang (1961: 28) describes the result of this attitude on the environs of a traditional Chinese dwelling:

> The influence of religion on the Chinese family life was everywhere visible. Upon entering any house, one saw paper door gods... painted on the doors for protection... On the floor was an alter to [*Tudi*], the earth god... [*Tian Guan*], the heavenly official, was in the courtyard, and the wealth gods, who brought well-being and prosperity to the family, were in the hall in the main room of the house....

In addition to the gods and the various religious movements, ancestor worship exerted its towering presence over family life. This form of homage was the one universal and unifying Chinese religious institution. Ancestor worship fostered a binding relationship between the living and the dead, the former to offer sacrifices and the latter to bestow blessings. With such a powerful institution whose figures lived on in heaven and wielded their authority on earth, it is no wonder that the idea of immortality found fertile ground to grow.

The belief in immortality cut a wide swath across the various philosophical, religious, and social camps in Chinese history. Emperors, peasants, merchants, and soldiers could share a belief in and the possibility of attaining eternal life. This was possible because religion in China encouraged a dynamic flow between its multitudinous sects and groupings that was unknown in the West. In Europe, one was a Catholic, a Protestant, a Jew, or a Moslem. An individual could not claim allegiance to more than one religious persuasion simultaneously. In contrast, the Chinese usually did not belong to a specific group nor were they required to profess loyalty to a particular article of faith. Professor Laurence Thompson (1989: 2) observed:

> Except in the case of the professional living apart in monasteries, religion in China was so woven into the broad fabric of family and social life that there was not even a special word for it (religion) until modern times, when one was coined to match the Western term.

Even the strict and uncompromising Confucians were not immune to the lure of immortality. Only the Buddhists, whose faith contained the doctrine of achieving *nirvana* or ego extinction, were unsympathetic to the transfiguration of the ego-self. Nevertheless, the Buddhists also allowed for a kind of immortality in the doctrine of reincarnation.

Of the many religious ideas, beliefs, and superstitions, the notion of immortality held a prominent and inspirational position in Chinese society, much like heaven in Western religions. Chinese folklore is filled with the stories of immortals who live forever and obtain supernatural powers such as walking through walls, flying through the air, and communing with the dead. These immortals often returned to earth to right wrongs and play tricks on the unwary. The Daoist sage Zhuangzi (third century BCE) drew a vivid portrait of one such immortal:

> There is a Holy Man living on faraway [*Gu-She*] mountain, with skin like ice or snow, and gentle and shy like a young girl. He doesn't eat the five grains, but sucks the wind, drinks the dew, climbs up on the clouds and mist, rides a flying dragon, and wanders beyond the four seas. By concentrating his spirit, he can protect creatures from sickness and plague and make the harvest plentiful.
>
> – Watson, 1964: 27

The following tale is a typical tale of immortality, with a moral to boot:

> There once lived a man who claimed to have discovered the secret of immortality. A Daoist priest decided to seek him out in order to be his disciple. When he reached the immortal's abode, he discovered that the man was dead. The priest was greatly disappointed and left immediately in great despair. Why was the priest disappointed? Was it because the man had departed from this life? But to become immortal, one must first die.
>
> – adapted from Van Over, 1984: 197

Significantly, the influence of immortality spilled over into the martial arts. The immortal and Daoist priest, Zhang Sanfeng, is the legendary founder of taijiquan. One tale recounted that he was meditating in a cave when the principles and postures of taiji came to him in a dream. Another version claimed that the postures suddenly appeared on the wall.

Zhang Sanfeng reputedly lived two hundred years in his physical body and then flew off to heaven as an immortal. It was said that a Daoist monk taught him the techniques of immortality when he dwelled and meditated in the Wudang Mountains, probably the site of his cave experience. During his mortal life, he performed many miracles and feats of strength that grew out of his knowledge of the shamanistic arts (Breslow, 1995: 200-209).

Ink rubbing of the
legendary founder of
taijiquan, Zhang Sanfeng.

The Origins of the Immortality Cult

The Chinese cult of immortality differed from the way people in the West generally viewed immortality. In Western religions, one lived forever and earned the reward of heaven by, for example, believing in the Divinity; performing good deeds; and, in some cases, through predetermined selection. In China, those who sought immortality had to harmonize their mental and physical life force with the eternal life force of the cosmos. To achieve their goal, they developed a vast array of spiritual practices and alchemical formulas.

Historically, the example of the legendary Yellow Emperor (*Huangdi*) became the paradigm for attaining immortality. While presiding over China's legendary Golden Age (2852-2255 BCE), not only did he teach the people how to use fire, plow their fields, and harvest the thread of the silk worm, but he also devoted his considerable talents and resources to acquiring the secret of eternal life. By virtue of his interest in medicine and in nourishing his own vitality, it was a logical step for the Yellow Emperor to seek immortality.[1] He reputedly experimented with metals and herbs and eventually found the formula for the golden elixir of immortality. After taking the drug, he mounted a dragon and flew away to the world of the immortals. Some legends note that he took his entire household of seventy people with him. Because such a revered figure as the Yellow Emperor was linked to immortality, it was difficult for later philosophers to deny its existence outright.

Following in the wake of the Yellow Emperor, the *fangshi* (magicians) were the keepers of the secret of immortality. These shamans practiced many mystical arts, such as astrology, spiritual healing, and divination. The general populace believed in their powers to achieve immortality, heal the sick, and perform miracles. Occasionally, the fangshi obtained the patronage of the ruling class. One famous emperor, Qin Shi Huangdi (259-210 BCE) sent a famous fangshi on a quest to find the "Isle of Immortals" and to bring back the elixir of immortality. He equipped a sea-faring expedition of three thousand men and women with ample supplies to accompany the shaman. They never returned. One legend recorded that they found the isle of immortality and decided to remain there as immortals. Another tale averred that they found the Japanese islands where the shaman crowned himself king and established a kingdom with his retinue. As for the hapless emperor, he used to wander along the shore, gazing at the eastern horizon in the hope of spotting the returning expedition.

Laozi and Immortality

From the third century BCE, several streams of Daoism flourished. While certain later branches of Daoism became identified as seekers of eternal life, other Daoists did not focus their efforts on achieving immortality. On the other hand, all Daoists shared a reverence for the Yellow Emperor and the heritage of Laozi (sixth century BCE) as their historical sources. Daoists were often called Huang-Lao because they were followers of both the Yellow Emperor and Laozi.

Fung Yu-lan, the great twentieth-century philosopher and historian, wrote that the best way to understand Daoism is to divide it into two distinct movements: philosophical Daoism (*Dao jia*) and religious Daoism (*Dao jiao*). Philosophical Daoists accepted certain ideas of Laozi, such as Dao being the creative life force of the universe, a love of nature, and a rejection of war. On the other hand, religious Daoists transformed Laozi's ideas into an all-inclusive belief system, with the *Daodejing*, his masterpiece, as their bible (Fung, 1966: 3).

If the Yellow Emperor was the mythical inspiration for Daoism, Laozi was its intellectual progenitor. Writing in his enigmatic, and at times indecipherable, style, Laozi advocated that the sage must strive to comprehend the mysterious workings of heaven and earth, that is, the Dao. Then, once these laws were understood as well as humanly possible, the sage must bring himself into harmony with them.

Laozi was aware that knowing the Dao was no easy task. In the first chapter of the *Daodejing*, Laozi informed his reader that the Dao cannot be named, that it is mysterious, and that it is "darkness within darkness."[2] Yet this mysterious Dao held within it the secret of life, for it was life itself. Furthermore, the Dao was "eternal." Thus, later seekers of immortality claimed that the sage who unraveled the secrets of the Dao secured for himself the possibility of merging with it and attaining the gift of eternal life.

At the Hui Shan Clay Figure Workshop in Wuxi city craftspeople create Daoist images, such as Laozi on a water buffalo (top) and the figurines adorned with longevity symbols such as the medicinal gourd, crane, and long beards. Much of the art reflects ideas associated with immortality. Photos by M. DeMarco.

In the *Daodejing*, Laozi did not speak explicitly on the subject of immortality. Nevertheless, his words, often closer to poetry than a cogent philosophy, profoundly influenced those Daoists seeking immortality. They interpreted his work to show that he indeed believed in immortality, pointing to several passages to support their claim. In Chapter 33, for example, Laozi declared:

> He who stays where he is endures.
> To die but not to perish
> Is to be eternally present.

According to religious Daoists, proper cultivation of the Dao would allow a sage to live eternally, even after death. However, many other commentators, like the great taiji master Zheng Manqing, interpreted this phrase differently. According to Professor Zheng, even though the sage dies, his contribution to humanity (his Dao) lived on.[3] In other words, his reputation and good deeds remained as his living testament.[4]

Another example where the religious Daoists uncovered the idea of immortality was found in Chapter 50. Laozi wrote:

> Rhinoceroses can find no place
> To thrust their horns,
> Tigers no place to use their claws,[5]
> And weapons no place to pierce.
> Why is this so?
> Because he has no place for death to enter.

It is noteworthy that Fung Yu-lan argued that the doctrine of immortality contradicted the spirit of Laozi and his writings (Fung, 1966: 3). Laozi believed that human beings should follow in the "natural" course of things (Feng and English, 1972: ch. 25). Life was followed by death and the sage should calmly accept this reality with cold indifference. On the other hand, religious Daoists focused their efforts on achieving immortality, which was the avoidance of death and, therefore, unnatural.

The *Daodejing* also provided the intellectual and inspirational wellspring for taijiquan practitioners. The book elaborated on the themes of yin and yang, *wuwei* (no unnatural action), and the relationship of hard and soft.[6] In Chapter 43, Laozi postulated: "The softest thing in the universe overcomes the hardest thing in the universe." This idea forms the pivot on which the entire system of taiji stands. Without this principle, one is not practicing taiji but something else. As the Buddhists were fond of saying: "Do not be fooled. A brass monkey may look like a gold monkey, but it is still made of brass."

Significantly, in Laozi, it is possible to see the confluence of taiji principles with the ideas of immortality. In Chapter 76, he observed:

> ... the stiff and unbending is the disciple of death.
> The gentle and yielding is the disciple of life.

Both practitioners of taiji and seekers of immortality focused on the positive value of life as opposed to death. Each required a gentle touch; patience; sensitivity; and, at times, a merging of one's personal ego with the greater Dao.

While Laozi's words were easily interpreted in various ways, he remains a seminal figure in the historiography of immortality and taiji. His pithy insights formed the intellectual framework for both the cults of immortality and the soft-styles of martial arts that followed him.

Public Morality Versus Immortality

Not everyone wholeheartedly accepted the doctrine of immortality. Its opponents often cloaked their dispute in evasive language, seldom attacking the popular precept head-on. In this debate, what was not said was of equal importance to what was. This was the case with Confucius, the most influential of all Chinese teachers.

Like Laozi, Confucius (or *Kongfuzi* in Chinese-Mandarin, 551-479 BCE) did not speak about immortality directly. Rather, he focused his attention elsewhere on the Dao of humanity. He was concerned about public morality in the here and now. This meant that he stressed the principles of righteousness, justice, and benevolence; and urged his students to weave these teachings into the moral fabric of normative society. Essentially, he was a social reformer, a radical conservative who wanted his followers to return to the traditional ways of the Chinese classics. The following represents his down-to-earth view of the spirit world:

> [Ji Lu] asked about serving the spirits of the dead.
> The Master said: "If you are not able to serve men,
> How can you serve their spirits?"
> [Ji Lu] added, "I venture to ask about death?"

He was answered, "While you do not know life,
How can you know about death?" – Legge, 1971: 241-42

and

The subjects on which the Master did not talk were—
extraordinary things, feats of strength, disorder,
and spiritual beings. – Legge, 1971: 201

The fact that he did not speak about "spiritual beings" and immortality suggests that, at the very least, he found the ideas problematic. His silence would be something like Thomas Jefferson refusing to comment on an important article in the Bill of Rights. Yet, in an interesting twist of logic, some later Daoists claimed that Confucius knew more about the spirit world than anyone else precisely because he did not speak about it (Fung, 1966: 219).

Other philosophers, who followed Confucius, also preferred to ignore the issue of immortality. Yang Xing (53 BCE-18 CE), a philosopher who combined Daoism with Confucianism, was asked to expound on the "actual truth" about immortals. He observed: "I shall have nothing to do with the question (of immortals). Their existence or nonexistence is not something to talk about. What should be asked are questions on loyalty and filial piety" (Chan, 1973: 290). In public, similar to Confucius, Yang believed that the sage should teach the Dao of humanity, presumably to establish a just and benevolent society. Notice that he did not deny the existence of immortals. Rather he preferred to deflect the question while emphasizing the Dao of humanity.

The Outer Elixir

The path to immortality was divided into two streams with different emphasis and methods: the outer elixir (*waidan*) and the inner elixir (*neidan*). The two were not mutually exclusive, although the inner elixir gradually became the method of choice for the vast majority of Daoists. It is interesting to note that the inner and outer method is the same classification used in defining the two major schools of qigong

To understand the mechanism of immortality, we must grasp the following important concept. The seekers of both the outer and inner schools believed that a person's *qi*, or lifeforce, was composed of the same stuff as the "eternal" cosmic qi of the universe. According to most Chinese thinkers, everything had its origins in the cosmic qi of Dao, which was something like the mountain water source of a great river (Feng and English, 1972: ch. 42).[7]

The great Neo-Confucian Zhang Zai (1020-1077) explained the unity of qi in this manner:

> When it is understood that the Vacuity, the Void, is nothing but material force (*qi*), then existence and nonexistence, the hidden and the manifested, spirit and eternal transformation, and human nature and destiny are all one and not a duality.[8]　　　　　– Chan, 1973: 502

Outer school followers sought to produce the pill of immortality from metals and herbs through alchemical processes.[9] Their goal was to bridge and unify the apparent duality of human qi and cosmic qi. The difference between the two qis was one of appearance, such as water, steam, and ice: their essence, or qi, was the same—H_2O. These pioneers of the modern laboratory scientist believed that a pill of gold and cinnabar combined with other ingredients, such as lead and water, would restore, balance, and harmonize an individual's personal qi with the cosmic qi. Cinnabar (red mercury ore) and gold were touted as the key ingredients of the elixir because they contained unique qualities of indestructibility and endurance.

The best known alchemist of the outer school was Ge Hong (284-364). He wrote the *Baopuzi*, a how-to book detailing specific techniques and practices for attaining immortality (Breslow, 1995: 132-33; Cooper, 1990; Schuhmacher and Woerner, 1989: 183). Ge Hong believed that only the pill of immortality could fulfill the promise of eternal life. Physical exercise, sexual yoga, breathing techniques, and meditation could prolong life but could not bestow the gift of immortality. Moreover, the pill could grant supernatural powers such as the ability to walk on water or to commune with the spirit world.

A monk descends Geling Hill which overlooks Hangzhou city.
Here, near a Daoist monastery, alchemist Ge Hong was believed
to have made pills for attaining immortality. Photo by M. DeMarco.

However, the pill alone could not produce immortality. Despite his belief in the elixir's magic, Ge Hong was also a committed Confucian. In order to achieve immortality, the practitioner had to practice the Confucian virtues of filial piety, good deeds, loyalty, trustworthiness, and sincerity. This is an interesting point because Ge Hong viewed immortality differently from Confucius and Yang Xing who refused to talk about immortals. It also highlights a Chinese worldview that emphasized the unity of mind and body. The wholeness of the person—spiritual, physical, and moral—was required in order to achieve immortality. A thief, for example, could imbibe the elixir of immortality and not achieve eternal life due to his character deficiencies.

The Inner Elixir

By the Song Dynasty (960-1279), the quest for the elixir of immortality became increasingly understood in spiritual rather than physical terms. In part, this evolution might be attributed to the lack of verifiable success regarding the outer school's approach.[10] Then, too, Neo-Confucian rationalists, such as Cheng Yi and Zhu Xi, who came to dominate Chinese thought from the tenth century CE, did not take kindly to the notion of immortality. The rise of Buddhism was another factor. Because of its highly sophisticated meditation techniques, Buddhism challenged both Daoism and Confucianism to develop their own equally skilled methods of contemplation, which many seekers then applied to achieving immortality.

Internal gongfu, including meditative and qigong practices,
are now practiced worldwide. Photo courtesy of the
Government Information Office, Taiwan, Republic of China.

The objective of Daoist spiritual yoga was the liberation of the yang soul (*shen*) from the hindrance of the yin or gross physical body. Traditionally, the Chinese understood that this separation occurred with death, but the Daoists came to believe it could happen while one lived. Taking their cue and terminology from the outer school, they sought to transform the body into an alchemical laboratory. For example, one early spiritual alchemy master explained that the semen corresponded to lead, blood to mercury, kidneys to water, and the mind to fire. By mixing these elements together, the meditator created the elixir of immortality in the fiery cauldron of his own body.

Gradually, the inner school rejected the outer school's terminology and developed its own framework known as the three treasures: *jing* (essence), *qi* (vitality), and *shen* (spirit). Each of the three treasures had two parts, an abstract and a concrete dimension:

	Concrete	**Abstract**	**Body**
Jing (essence):	male sperm and female sexual fluids	creativity as the seed of life	genitals
Qi (vitality):	air and breath	internal energy and life force	stomach, dantian
Shen (spirit):	ordinary conscious, thoughts and feelings	spiritual consciousness	lungs, head, and heart

To preserve life and to attain immortality, the three treasures had to be conserved and blended into a balanced harmony. Through daily nourishment, seekers of the inner elixir sought to cultivate the natural growth of the three treasures. For example, the breath was not merely a means for maintaining life. If it was not regulated properly, the person's lifeforce would be used up. Conversely, correct breathing techniques would greatly increase the lifeforce in the body.

Ejaculation was another example of body ecology and conservation. Daoists seeking immortality believed that the semen represented a major source of qi and had to be preserved within the body, particularly as one grew older.[11] During the act of lovemaking, the male would prevent ejaculation through various techniques, thereby sending the semen (*jing*) back through the spinal passage as refined life force (*qi*) and to the brain, where it nourished the spirit (*shen*).

Daoist seekers of immortality believed that the bodily processes and functions normally leading to death could be "reversed" by concentrating and purifying the three treasures.[12] By reversing the life-to-death process with various meditation and visualization techniques, one could return to his or her "pre-birth" state and transform the coarse body into subtle energy. This was the same principle utilized in sexual yoga: the transmuting of *jing* into qi and then qi into *shen*.

Qigong exercises and taijiquan were important vehicles to improve health and, for some, to attain immortality. These kinds of exercises were highly valued because they conserved and strengthened the body's life force, allowing the qi to flow evenly and freely along the spine to the head.

The taiji classics adopted the same principle used in immortality, which became a hallmark in its concept of self-defense. The taiji classics extolled the principle of the "suspended head top" to promote a light and responsive body: "When the *ching shen* [*jing shen*] (spirit) is raised, there is no fault of stagnancy and heaviness" (Lo, et al., 1985: 47). In other words, the body reacts quickly and appropriately to the attack of an opponent because mind and posture have allowed the *jing* and qi to flow freely and to become *shen* (Breslow, 1995: 282-83, 299).

A monk stands in front of the Hall of the Eight Immortals.
He is a native of Guangzhou but came to live in Beijing's White Cloud Monastery, a leading center of Daoism in China. Photo by M. DeMarco.

Generally, to conserve their qi and prepare themselves for immortality, Daoists followed the Middle Path whereby they avoided excess in all things. Moderation was their by-word. Even Daoist exercises like qigong were kept within the bounds of common sense. One of my taiji teachers often reminded us to do our best but don't overdo it. The following is a Daoist checklist on maintaining moderation:

1) excessive walking harms the nerves
2) excessive standing harms the bones
3) too much sleep harms the blood vessels
4) sitting too long harms the blood
5) listening too much impairs the generative powers
6) looking at things too long harms the spirit
7) talking too much affects the breath
8) thinking too hard upsets the stomach
9) too much sex injures the life force
10) eating too much damages the heart

—adapted from Cooper, 1990: 104

Taiji masters also recommended that their students should follow the path of moderation. The *Taiji Classics* state: "It is not excessive or deficient; Accordingly when it bends, It then straightens" (Lo, et al., 1985: 31).

Mr. Jiang Jialun, a member of the Hangzhou Wushan Taijiquan Association, in "Stork Spread Wings." This movement is found in taijiquan and qigong. Because it is associated with long life, many believe it is beneficial to move and breath like the bird. Photo by Donald Mainfort.

In practical terms, this meant that, whether practicing the taiji form or sparring with an opponent, one must hold to the center. "Excessive" indicates that one should not bend over too far and "deficient" means not to lose contact with the opponent (Wile, 1983: 117-18).

Pre-natal Breathing: A Practical Lesson

To understand the inner school theory, it might be helpful to examine a breathing technique called "prenatal" or "reverse" breathing. This technique is characterized by contracting the lower abdomen on the in-breath and expanding it on the out-breath. According to the Daoists, each baby is born with prenatal qi, which is the life force it receives before birth. Some babies are endowed with more qi than others, depending on the health of the parents, genetics, and other factors. Before the baby is born, he takes in his nourishment and oxygen through the umbilical cord and stores the energy in his dantian. Once the baby is born, breathing from the nose and mouth begins, which is known as "post-birth" breathing. This transition marks the end of prenatal breathing.

However, if we closely observe a baby breathing, we will see that, while he breathes through his nose, he still uses his stomach in the breathing process. We can actually observe the abdomen moving rhythmically with the breath. The Daoists noticed that, as one grows older, the diaphragm and abdomen are employed less and less. The breath gradually moves higher in the lungs until it flies out of the mouth, culminating in death.

The Daoists hoped to accomplish two goals with prenatal breathing. They wanted to reverse the upward pattern of the breath so that it would remain deep in the lower stomach, that is, in the dantian. In this way, it was thought that a person would not "expire." They accomplished this goal by harmonizing the movement of the abdomen and the breath.

Secondly, the Daoists believed that when one's qi was depleted the person died. Thus, if one could conserve, strengthen, and nourish the prenatal qi stored in the dantian, then he or she would never get sick and die. The Daoists hoped to accomplish this by mixing the qi from the air outside the body, a never-ending source, with the prenatal qi inside the body. This was done by simultaneously contracting the dantian and inhaling fresh air, joining them together in the area of the diaphragm, and then sending the revitalized qi back to its storage place in the dantian.

qi = 氣 • *dantian* = 丹田

Immortality At Last

One who attained immortality became a *xian*. The modern pictogram for a *xian* is made up of the pictograms for a man and a mountain, suggesting the correlation between the recluse and immortality. The earlier pictogram for xian showed a man ascending toward heaven. The best known immortals in Chinese mythology were the Eight Immortals (*ba xian*), who are often depicted in Chinese art. They represent the eight conditions of life: youth, old age, poverty, riches, nobility, common people, woman, and man.

Ge Hong divided immortals into three categories: celestial, terrestrial, and those who had given up the body. Celestial immortals fly to heaven with their bodies intact like the Yellow Emperor. Terrestrial immortals dwell in mountains or forests. Ge Hong's death was reputedly an example of the third kind. When he died, he was placed in a coffin. Later when the coffin was opened, only his clothes remained. This passing to the spirit world represented a cross-cultural, archetypal image, as it closely resembles the resurrection of Jesus of Nazareth in the New Testament.

In Chinese folklore, the types of immortals appear less clear than Ge Hong's definitions of the *xian*. Did the immortal one remain the same after achieving immortality, his or her qi having reached the point of indestructibility? Or did he or she die, dropping the physical body while the body/mind was transfigured into subtle energy? The answer was that the immortal could do and be just about anything he or she pleased. Whatever actually occurred, the immortal was viewed as a power technician of the highest rank. This meant that he could transform his body and environment to the shape of his will. The immortal often performed magic and miracles. This ability came from great personal power and a deep understanding of the way energy worked.

The following legends illustrate the above point and demonstrate the convergence of immortality with personal power and martial arts. When Zhang Sanfeng, the father of taijiquan, was on his way to the capital at the invitation of Emperor Huizong (1092-1135), he had to pass through mountains populated by dangerous bandits. That night, Yuandi, one of the semidivine immortals, visited him in a dream and taught him certain self-defense techniques. The following day, Zhang was attacked and he reputedly killed more than a hundred bandits.

Another story about Zhang describes his great personal power. Apparently, in winter, Zhang would walk out of the monastery to enjoy the hoary landscape. It was said that he left no footprints on the snowy paths. The legend does not say whether he flew or stepped down without leaving an indentation. Presumably, he could do either.

A scenic wonder in any season, Hangzhou city's West Lake has long inspired poets, emperors, and martial artists. People come daily to the shores to "run like tigers," hang upside down like bats from trees, and practice other assorted techniques in a quest for health and longlife. Photo by Donald Mainfort.

Immortality in the Modern Age

In the modern world, belief in the elixir of immortality has fallen by the wayside. Yet we have much to be thankful for its existence and those seekers who aimed for the stars but only reached the moon. For example, Fung Yu-lan praised religious Daoism as heralding the spirit of modern science. Daoist alchemists accumulated a massive body of medical lore and laid the basis for modern chemistry, metallurgy, botany, herbology, and zoology. Traditional Chinese medicine was also greatly beholden to the seekers of immortality.

The search for immortality gave impetus to the belief that human beings can live healthier, longer, and happier lives. It offered an ancient and well-tested structure of exercise, meditation, and visualization that enabled ordinary people to dramatically enhance the quality of their lives. While promising no guarantees regarding death and sickness, the Daoist health systems postulated that it is best to follow the Dao, to "walk like a cat" so that one might live as a lion in winter.[13] The taiji classics sum it up

73

best: "Think it over carefully what the final purpose is: to lengthen life and maintain youth" (Lo, et al.: 66).

In 1935 John Blofeld met a Daoist monk at his monastery in the mountains. This was what that monk had to say about immortals:

> Immortals not only break wind or belch like other people, they die... Becoming immortal has little to do with physical changes, like the graying of a once glossy black beard; it means coming to know something, realizing something—an experience that can happen in a flash! Ah, how precious is that knowledge! When it first strikes you, you want to sing and dance, or you nearly die of laughing! For suddenly you recognize that nothing in the world can hurt you. — Blofeld, 1979: 180

Notes

1. *The Yellow Emperor's Classic of Internal Medicine*, made up of the Yellow Emperor asking questions regarding health from his minister, Qi Po, forms the basis for traditional Chinese medical practices.

2. All translations of the *Daodejing* come from Feng and English.

3. Tam Gibbs translated the verse differently: "One who does not lose what he has gained is durable. One who dies yet remains has longevity" (Cheng, 1981: 119).

4. This idea is echoed in other cultures. In Judaism, there is this adage: "The righteous live through their deeds even though they are dead while the unrighteous are dead even though they live."

5. This phrase should be compared with the wonderful story Robert Smith (1997: 66-68) told when Professor Zheng encountered a tiger. Then, read the Professor's commentary on *Laozi* (the one we quoted in the text) in Wile (1985: 25).

6. I am often surprised how few practitioners of martial arts, particularly students of taiji, have studied Laozi's masterpiece in depth. It should be read and reread along with the *Taiji Classics* and Sunzi's, *The Art of War*.

7. The *Taiji Classics* also state this principle: "T'ai Chi [*taiji*] comes from *Wu Chi* [*wuji*] and is the mother of Yin and Yang" (Lo, et al., 1985: 31).

8. Many great martial artists drew on their harmony with cosmic qi for their spiritual inspiration and physical power. Witness the words of Morihei

Ueshiba, the founder of aikido:

> Regardless of how quickly an opponent attacks or how slowly I respond, I cannot be defeated... As soon as the thought of attack crosses my opponent's mind, he shatters the harmony of the universe and is instantly defeated regardless of how quickly he attacks. Victory or defeat is not a matter of time and space.
>
> – Stevens, 1987: 112

[9] We should be misled into thinking that the pill is part of the Inner School merely because it is ingested.

[10] How one verifies the existence of immortals or the success of such an endeavor is an interesting problem. Few mystics, East or West, are willing to put themselves to the test. Besides, spirits and immortals are known to be notoriously shy. Furthermore, the Daoists of both the Inner and Outer Schools were not interested in proving anything. They were simply doers, striving to achieve immortality, often recluses who were unconcerned with the cares of the world. They had nothing to prove.

[11] Su Nu, the Yellow Emperor's female advisor, suggested the following approach:

> When a man loves once without losing his semen, he will strengthen his body. If he loves twice without losing it, his hearing and vision will become more acute. If three times, all diseases may disappear. If four times, he will have peace of mind. If five times, his heart and blood circulation will be revitalized. If six times, his loins will become strong. If seven times, his buttocks and thighs may become more powerful. If eight times, his skin may become smooth. If nine times, he will become immortal.
>
> – Chang, 1977: 44

[12] Today, taiji and qigong teachers are more modest in their claims and tend to use the words "halting" or "arresting" the process of old age instead of "reversing it." Nevertheless, in some cases, I have seen people drop ten years by strengthening their qi.

Bibliography

Blofeld, J. (1979). *Taoism: The road to immortality*. Boulder: Shambhala Publications, Inc.

Breslow, A. (1995). *Beyond the closed door: Chinese culture and the creation of t'ai chi ch'uan*. Jerusalem, Israel: Almond Blossom Press.

Chan, W. (Trans.). (1963). *A source book in Chinese philosophy*. Princeton: Princeton University Press.

Chang, J. (1977). *The tao of love and sex: The ancient Chinese way to ecstasy*. New York: E. P. Dutton.

Cheng, M. (1981). *Lao tzu: My words are very easy to understand*. (T.C. Gibbs, Trans.). Berkeley, CA: North Atlantic Books.

Cohen, K. (1997). *The way of qigong: The art and science of Chinese energy healing*. New York: Ballentine Books.

Cooper, J. (1990). *Chinese alchemy: The Taoist quest for immortality*. New York: Sterling Publications.

Schuhmacher, S., and Woerner, G. (Eds.). (1989). *Encyclopedia of eastern philosophy and religion*. Boston: Shambhala Publications, Inc.

Feng, G., and English, J. (Trans.). (1972). *Tao te ching*. New York: Vintage Books.

Fung, Y. (1966). *A short history of Chinese philosophy*. (D. Bodde, Ed.). New York: The Free Press Edition.

Legge, J. (Trans.). (1971). *The Chinese classics, vol. 1: Confucian analects, the great learning, the doctrine of the mean*. New York: Dover Publications.

Lo, P., Inn, M., Amacker, R., and Foe, S. (Trans.). (1985). *The essence of t'ai chi ch'uan*. Berkeley, CA: North Atlantic Books.

Smith, R. (1997). Da lu and some tigers. *Journal of Asian Martial Arts*, 6(2), 56-69.

Stevens, J. (1987). *Abundant peace: The biography of Morihei Ueshiba, founder of aikido*. Boston: Shambhala Publications, Inc.

Thompson, L. (1989). *Chinese religion*. Belmont, CA: Wadsworth Publishing Company.

Van Over, R. (Ed.). (1984). *Taoist tales*. New York: Meridian.

Watson, B. (Trans.). (1968). *Chuang tzu: The inner chapters*. New York: Columbia University Press.

Wile, D. (Trans.). (1985). *Cheng Man-Ch'ing's advanced tai-chi form instructions with selected writings on meditation, the I Ching, medicine and the arts*. Brooklyn, NY: Sweet Ch'i Press.

Wile, D. (Trans.). (1983). *T'ai-chi touchstones: Yang family secret transmissions*. Brooklyn, NY: Sweet Ch'i Press.

Yang, C. (1961). *Religion in Chinese society*. Berkeley, CA: University of California Press.

· 5 ·

Reviving the Daoist Roots
of Internal Martial Arts
by Mark Hawthorne

Monk of the orthodox Complete Reality Sect. Photograph by Kipling Swehla.
Photos courtesy of the Taoist Restoration Society.

When Zhang Sanfeng began developing taijiquan as a comprehensive system of martial arts in the thirteenth century, this Daoist monk ensured his place in history as the first patriarch of the art. Of course, history can get muddled with the passing centuries, but Zhang is generally credited with synthesizing the philosophical principles of Daoism with a martial art that could be used for both self-defense and a method to enhance one's internal energy (qi). Thus, Daoist monks used taijiquan to defend themselves and as an exercise for the mind and body (Liang, 1996: 8-9).

Seven centuries later, taijiquan is still a popular martial art, both in China and around the world. But while the art has flowered into a global practice, its roots have been nearly destroyed, and Daoism exists only as a fragile remnant of the past or more a vestigial tradition than the vigorous philosophy and religion that was once one of China's most important belief systems. Whether or not Daoism can be revived may well depend on the efforts of those in China now struggling to rebuild the monasteries and temples and to bring back the clergy who once populated them.

The threat to Daoism began in the last century as the power of the Qing Dynasty (1644-1912) began to decline. As China became weak enough to be invaded by Western powers, many suspected the Daoists of plotting against the emperor, and imperial support began to drop. China finally shed its imperial dynasties and founded a Nationalist Government in 1912; gone were the powerful emperors who had long supported the Daoist monasteries and temples. The new government, which believed Daoism to be based on superstition and folklore, allowed the system to struggle on its own, and monasteries and temples fell into disrepair.

Photography by Kipling Swehla.

In 1949, Mao Zedong and his Communists toppled China's government and then outlawed Daoism altogether. They reasoned that an ideologically perfect state made religion unnecessary. Monasteries were destroyed or requisitioned as government buildings, and monks, nuns and Daoist officials were imprisoned in labor camps, reducing the clergy from several millions to about 50,000.

Today there is a new mind-set in China, a more liberal attitude that sees religious expression as an important part of traditional Chinese culture and a direct link to such martial arts as xingyiquan and taijiquan. Daoist sites must be restored, say supporters of this ancient tradition, and the clergy must be allowed to transmit their mystic teachings to the next generation. And thus the race to save Daoism, China's oldest indigenous religion, is on.

One group leading the work to rescue Daoism is the Taoist Restoration Society (TRS) (Taoist, 1999). Brock Silvers founded the nonprofit organization nine years ago after visiting China and seeing for himself how Daoism was threatened with extinction. "By the early 1980's," he says, "most Western scholars believed that Daoism had been effectively stamped out by China's modern upheavals. We thought Daoism was a dead religion" (personal communication, 1999).

Although based in the U.S., the TRS works out of Beijing to support the restoration of monastic institutions and assist Daoist communities. The organization works to rebuild Daoist sites for their original purpose, not as museums or tourist attractions. It also supports the revival of organized Daoism and is especially involved in the restoration of temples, almost all of which somewhere in the tens of thousands—were requisitioned or destroyed by the government.

The Chinese leadership has joined the effort with its own organization, the National Daoist Association (NDA), which officially oversees all Daoist activity in China. Headquartered in Beijing, the NDA runs the entire national Daoist organization. Its new director is Min Zhiting, a well-respected Daoist monk. These two groups, combined with the work of Daoist monks, nuns and other supporters, are working within what Silvers sees as a "ten year window of opportunity to save Daoism" (personal communication, 1999).

Dao of Daoism

Nature is the model that Daoists use as a guide for ideal behavior, including the practice of martial arts. By observing nature, we see that everything is in balance and governed by the same laws. By imitating nature, we learn to both survive and live in harmony. Hua Tuo (141-203 CE), a Chinese physician, introduced a system of renewing one's qi with a combination of mental, physical and breathing exercises called daoyin. He also created a system of exercises known as the Sport of the Five Animals, which seeks to imitate the speed, agility and power of such animals as the bear, crane, deer, monkey and tiger. From these exercises came Hua's Five Animal Games, regarded as the first system of martial arts in China (Breslow, 1995: 192-195).

Photography: left, by Brock Silvers, right, by Katherine McVety.

Daoism refers to both a philosophy (*Daojia*) and a religion (*Daojiao*) and is thought to have developed in China in the sixth and fifth centuries BCE. As a philosophy, Daoism stresses that one should not try to change the way things are—nature provides everything. Religious Daoism evolved from several philosophical and religious movements, and the first temple was founded in the second century CE. Religious Daoism incorporates the worship of many gods and a veneration of nature and simplicity. Because Daoists view the body and spirit as one, the goal is not to liberate the soul from the body but to nurture one's qi and attain the Dao by realizing the truth within you (Schumacher, 1996: 162-173).

Dao ("the Way") plays an important role in both religious and philosophical Daoism. It is concerned with the course of events and order of the universe. It is an intangible reality that gives rise to existence. All things, in time, return to the Dao. Dao may also be understood as "the Way things do what they do." There is a Way to do everything, and once you master that, you need not be concerned with it. For example, after learning the Way to ride a bicycle, the rider doesn't have to think about it; he simply does it. Practitioners of Daoism attempt to gain mystical union with the Dao through meditation and by following the nature of the Dao in thought and action (Schumacher, 1996: 163-166).

The Dao is a principal feature of two classic Daoist texts, the *Daodejing* (The Book of the Way and Its Power) and the *Zhuangzi*. Many scholars credit authorship of the *Daodejing* to Laozi, the Chinese philosopher believed to have lived in the the sixth century BCE. Although the book's origin is in debate, it forms the basis of both religious and philosophical Daoism. The Daoist sage Zhuangzi (c. 369-286 BCE) is regarded as the author of the text by the same name. The Zhuangzi's views on Dao, *de* ("power") and *wuwei* ("non-doing" or "inaction") mirror those of the *Daodejing* (Schumacher, 1996: 210-211).

Wuwei is an important tenet in martial arts. Inaction finds its power within the individual and his understanding of the nature of all things. It is a natural law for all things to always be what they are—interfere with this law and you have failed. Challenges are to be ignored, says the *Daodejing*, and *wuwei* is the only means of achieving true success (Barrett, 1993: 28). Compare these principles with the efficacy of redirecting an opponent's attack, allowing him to be thrown off-guard and conquered by his own inertia.

Yin-yang is another central aspect of Daoism. These two contradictory yet complementary energies are said to be the cause of the universe and represent the duality of existence. Yin and yang are manifestations of the Dao of the supreme ultimate, or the Supreme One, which is known in Chinese as *taiji* (*taijiquan* translates as the "fist of the supreme ultimate"). Yin is feminine, receptive and soft. Yang is masculine, creative and hard. While *yin* symbolizes the moon, shadows, death and earth, *yang* represents the sky, light, life and fire. These two polarities are in constant fluctuation, with one side dominating and then yielding to the other. Nothing is ever purely yin or yang; all things are comprised of varying degrees of both. A cloud, for example, might be yin because it is soft and yang because it is white (Schumacher, 1996: 216-219).

Photography by Kipling Swehla.

Dao of Martial Arts

Although taijiquan might seem the most obvious connection, the Daoist tenets of yielding and softness have given birth to other martial arts, especially the "internal" styles. In Daoist spiritual training the internal martial arts are used for both spiritual development and external power. The four internal styles are bagua, xingyiquan, liuhebafa and taijiquan (Wong, 1997: 226).

"The differences between external and internal martial arts do not arise from specific techniques employed by the various styles," says Wai Lun Choi, who teaches internal martial arts in Chicago, Illinois. "The differences stem from the way the movements are produced. External styles emphasize speed and power, but this is also true of the internal arts. What really differentiates them are the training methods used to develop this speed and power. Internal styles require a precise unity of breathing, weight distribution, joint alignment, leverage, etc., any time a movement is executed" (personal communication, 1999).

Bagua ("Eight Trigrams," refers to heaven, earth, water, fire, thunder, wind, mountain and lake) most likely grew from Daoism in the seventeenth century into a variety of systems practiced around the world today. The bagua boxing style uses fluid motions and swift footwork, moving in circles to confuse the opponent. The victor outflanks his rival, remaining safely behind or beside the source of danger. Bagua demands exceptional concentration (Wong, 1997: 226-227).

Photography by Kipling Swehla.

82

Xingyiquan ("Form and Intention Fist") is attributed to Yue Fei, a twelfth century Chinese general. Although he helped popularize it, Yue credited a wandering Daoist with teaching him the art. As with many legends, its accuracy is questionable (others date the art to the Shaolin Temple in the sixth century), but xingyiquan remains very martial in appearance, characterized by pounding, thrusting and hitting with bursts of movement. Xingyiquan is efficient in its expression of power, with the practitioner using a full range of body motions for grappling, locking, throwing and trapping techniques (Wong, 1997: 227).

Liuhebafa ("Six Harmonies and Eight Methods") is probably the least known of the internal martial arts, at least in the West. This art blends elements of taiji, bagua and xingyiquan. "Unlike the other three internal arts," says Wai Lun Choi, "liuhebafa uses over 700 different techniques. The art rests on a foundation of biology, physiology and anatomy, and the spirit enables its proper performance. Its theory, from every perspective, complies with what is practical and scientifically sound. To develop yourself, you must turn away from mysticism and the belief in secrets you imagine will transform you. Science and nature are your true teachers and correct training is what will transform you" (personal communication, 1999).

Taijiquan, perhaps the most popular of the internal arts founded on Daoism, is a subtle system practiced today primarily for its health benefits. The style, which seeks to cultivate one's qi, finds maximum efficiency through integrating the mind and body in harmonious movement. *Qi* is described as that through which the Dao manifests itself and then differentiates into two forces—yin and yang. Taijiquan practitioners use the doctrine of yin and yang throughout their training. In push-hands practice, for example, it is only by achieving softness and yielding to the opponent's attack that he is effectively repelled (Kauz, 1997: 60). "Most of the traditional internal martial arts training is still underground in China and was so long before Mao," says Dr. Yang Jwing-Ming, author and martial arts instructor for more than thirty years. "These arts have been considered top secret since ancient times when they were taught mainly in the monasteries. Even then, they were taught with the goal of spiritual enlightenment." All that changed in 1911.

"Beginning in the late Qing Dynasty, and continuing for some time afterward, the knowledge of internal martial arts was gradually revealed to people outside the monastic community. But then the Communist party took over and they started to control the martial arts community and kept the real martial arts suppressed, fearing the martial artists would unite against the party rule. Combat techniques in martial arts training have been gradually neglected in China ever since" (personal communication, 1999).

Dr. Yang, who was raised in Taiwan and has lived in the U.S. for 25 years, believes there is only one way to keep the internal martial arts alive. "I visited mainland China recently," he says, "and I was surprised to learn that no one under fifty even understands the relationship between qi and the *jin*—that is, internal power. There is still some traditional training in the Chinese countryside, but only a small number of traditional practitioners. I realized the only way to preserve the internal arts was to teach them outside of China" (personal communication, 1999).

Photography by Kipling Swehla.

Although Daoism's link to external martial arts is more difficult to establish, a case can be made that many of these arts are indebted to the central Daoist principle of the duality of opposites. Indeed, probably any style that advocates fluid motion, yielding responses and avoiding or redirecting an opponent's attack can claim Daoism as its inspiration. As the *Daodejing* says:

Rushing into action, you fail.
Trying to grasp things, you lose them.
Forcing a project to completion,
You ruin what was almost ripe.
– Mitchell. 1991: 64

Daoism Today

TRS and NDA would like to ensure that every major city in China has at least one major Daoist place of worship. Although there is no official restoration plan, major Daoist sites have been the first to be renovated, a task that often involves a construction company. Smaller projects are usually handled by Daoist clergy, often with the assistance of volunteers from the lay community. While the government pays for its own projects, funds for much of the other reconstruction come from supporters throughout Asia, Europe and the United States. The final cost of a restoration varies widely: anywhere from a few hundred U.S. dollars to several million, depending on the size of the site and extent of damage.

Photography by Kipling Swehla.

Silvers notes that it is difficult to control the use of Daoist iconography and symbols. "From what I have seen," he says, "the government doesn't really care about authenticity. And even those who do care—officials and monks alike—are often hampered by a combination of poverty and ignorance" (personal communication, 1999). Which is why TRS not only helps fund projects, but puts pressure on the Chinese government to use greater care as sites are being rebuilt.

The government's National Daoist Association and local religious affairs bureaus across China are also working to save the tradition from extinction, with varying degrees of success. Last January, for example, the government opened a renovated temple dedicated to the god of Tai Shan. The ancient temple, one of the largest in Beijing, was a favorite of the Qing emperors and was rebuilt by a local tourist bureau. Thus, rather than being renovated as a place of worship, the temple now stands as a cultural museum and no Daoist clergy are allowed to engage in religious activity there.

Photography by Katherine McVety.

Daoism Tomorrow

With so many people working on national and local levels toward a goal that is paramount to preserving China's culture, it is tempting to believe that the fight to save Daoism is won. After all, if it's something everyone wants, why the struggle? But turning the tide on a century of destruction is not a simple matter.

The good news is that the restoration of Daoism seems to be taking hold, with major temples crowded on holidays, new sites being constructed and the quality of renovations constantly improving. People throughout China have been very receptive to their reborn Daoist traditions, with more and more viewing themselves as Daoist. But it will take more than renovated temples and contented practitioners to ensure Daoism's survival. As Silvers explains:

> ... The real window of opportunity involves the expected life spans of the old, pre-Communist generation of clergy—the 'laodao' masters— who are generally seventy to one hundred years old. With each temple that is restored or reactivated, more *laodao* are recalled from the fields, the retired workers' hospitals or any kind of work unit to which they might have been assigned.

Although these *laodao* are not numerous, they have embraced the task of breeding a new generation of religious seekers and leaders. It is imperative that organized Daoism reclaims its heritage before the current supply of *laodao* passes away. When these adepts pass away, the previous Daoist age will go with them. – personal communication, 1999

These *laodao* (elder Daoists) include China's many martial arts masters, whose teachings were suppressed under the threat of imprisonment and death during Mao's reign. The progressive decline of China's traditional martial arts is also a loss to the world, where the destruction of any cultural expression is disgraceful.

Adds Silvers (personal communication, 1999): "It would certainly be a tragedy to witness the functional extinction of the tradition which gave so much impetus and energy to the early development of the internal martial arts. The internal arts and Daoism will forever be linked; can one really be whole without the other?"

Photography by Kipling Swehla.

Mindful that Chinese President Jiang Zemin already has his hands full, Silvers remains hopeful. "Things are already so much better than they were ten or twenty years ago," he says. "Average Han Chinese people do have more religious freedom than their parents did. And the human soul abhors a vacuum. But traditions and places and rituals and songs and prayers and the like are being forgotten every day. Half a religion probably can't survive. But we might succeed yet" (personal communication, 1999).

Bibliography

Barred, T. (1993). *Dao: To know and not be knowing*. San Francisco, CA: Chronicle Books.

Breslow, A. (1995). *Beyond the closed door: Chinese culture and the creation of t'ai chi ch'uan*. Jerusalem, Israel: Almond Blossom Press.

Chuang-Tzu. (1998). *The essential Chuang-Tzu*. (S. Hamill and J.P. Seaton, Trans.). Boston, MA: Shambala Publications.

Frantiz, B. (1998). *The power of internal martial arts: Combat secrets of bagua, tai chi and hsing-i*. Berkeley, CA: North Atlantic Books.

Kauz, H. (1997). *Push hands: The handbook for noncompetitive tai chi practice with a partner*. Woodstock, NY: The Overlook Press.

Liang, S. (1996). *Tai chi chuan*. Rosindale, MA: YMAA Publication Center.

Mitchell, S. (1991). *Tao te ching*. New York, NY: HarperPerennial.

Schumacher, S., and Woerner, G. (1996). *Shambala dictionary of Daoism*. Boston, MA: Shambala Publications.

Taoist Restoration Society (1999). http://www.taorestore.com.

Wong, E. (1997). *The Shambala guide to Daoism*. Boston, MA: Shambala Publications.

· 6 ·

Ge Hong: Famous Daoist Thinker and Practical Martial Artist

by Stanley E. Henning, M.A.

While in the military, Ge Hong killed two pursuers and a horse with archery from horseback. The illustration is from a 1609 edition of *Comprehensive Illustrated Encyclopedia* (*Sancai Tuhui*). Courtesy of the University of Hawaii, Hamilton Library.

Ge Hong, also named Zhichuan (Youthful River) and Baopuzi (One Who Embraces Simplicity) (283-363 CE), known primarily for his Daoist pursuits, was not only an important intellectual figure of his time, but also a military officer versed in martial arts. Although he only offers a few short lines on the subject in all his writings, they reveal valuable insights into the place of martial arts in society and aspects of their practice through the ages to modern times.

Ge Hong was a fascinating individual: a combination Confucian, Legalist, and Daoist intellectual, military officer, and official who had practiced martial arts and experienced combat, and a Daoist recluse and alchemist. In sum, his philosophy was to cultivate the inner saint and perfect the outer prince; to seek immortality through good works, other Daoist practices including alchemy, and improve the world by implementing the moral and legal way.

In the "Outer Chapters" of his *Baopuzi*, Ge Hong discusses success and failure in human affairs and what is permissible in matters belonging to the realm of Confucianism. It is no accident that he mentions martial arts in his postscript to this section as opposed to the "Inner Chapters," which he dedicates to Daoist pursuits. Ge Hong may actually be reflecting satire within his self-effacing tone that contrasts his own postscript to the "Outer Chapters" with that of Three Kingdom's Emperor Wei Wendi's (a.k.a. Cao Pi, 187-226 CE) postscript to *Discussing the Classics* (*Dian Lun*).[1] He notes that the Emperor's purpose was to speak of things he knew, such as archery, chess and fencing in which he was adept, while Ge Hong, on the contrary, claims to speak of things that he is not good at, including martial arts.

The Emperor boasts about his archery skills in hunting and his demonstration at a feast with a stick of sugar cane as a sword to thrice defeat General Deng Zhan's famed bare-hand-against-weapons fighting skills.[2] Ge Hong, on the other hand, merely notes in passing that he is not as skilled as young boys in throwing tiles and boxing (basic martial arts skills) and that, although he was not particularly strong in drawing a bow, he once had to use his mounted archery to kill two men and a horse to save his skin. He notes that archery was one of the Six Arts (Confucian disciplines including rites, music, mathematics, writing, charioteering and archery) that could also be used to defend against bandits or for hunting. He then notes that he had studied broadsword and shield, single-handed broadsword and double halberds and, later in life, seven foot staff with which one could counter the blade of the large halberd. Finally, he explains that all the martial arts have secret formulas to describe important techniques and secret, mysterious methods to overcome an opponent. If an opponent was unaware of these one could defeat him every time. In other words, Ge Hong was no mere novice.

When pieced together, Ge Hong's comments in his postscript to the *Baopuzi Outer Chapters* along with Emperor Wei Wendi's postscript to *Discussing the Classics*, which Ge Hong references, provide a panoramic view of the martial arts in Chinese society of his time. To begin with, we can see that the martial arts were widely practiced in one form or another at all levels and by all elements of society, from leaders to the commoners who formed militias. Even the literati were familiar with archery, one of the Six Arts they were expected to learn. Among various forms of play, many young males practiced boxing and the martial arts related sport of tile/stone tossing (for accuracy and distance).[3] These arts were practiced as worldly, not religious or spiritual activities, as Ge Hong clearly reflects. Later sources reveal that martial arts were practiced in Buddhist monasteries as well, after all, monks also came from society at large, and monastic property needed to be protected, especially in times of famine and political unrest. In any case, Ge Hong lived over 100 years prior to the founding of Shaolin Monastery, most well-known for its later association with the martial arts.

As for the incident between Emperor Wei Wendi and General Deng Zhan, the latter's touted ability to defeat an armed opponent using his bare hands is an example of what boxing was really all about in those days—basic training for use of weapons, to assist in the use of weapons in some cases, and to use as a last resort when one was weaponless.[4]

Last but not least, Ge Hong refers to the role of oral formulas (*koujue*) and secret methods (*mifa*) to support martial arts practices. These were mnemonic devices (common to the Chinese learning process of memorization) that provided insights on proper technique in practice. Ge Hong emphasizes that the techniques described in these oral formulas and/or secret methods can be effective if the opponent does not know them (they describe fighting tactics and techniques). They were often unintelligible or unclear to those outside the particular group that used them in training. They were brought to life by the hands-on instruction of one's teacher.

Ge Hong's concise, matter of fact comments on martial arts practices in his time provide us one of the best descriptions ever written. This description is, in turn, a key to our understanding of the role of the martial arts in Chinese society over the centuries. As for Ge Hong himself, he spent his final years in seclusion, seeking the path to immortality through alchemy at Mount Luofu outside Guangzhou.

Glossary

Baopuzi 抱朴子
Cao Pi 曹丕
Cefu Yuangui 冊府元龜
dan dao 單刀
Deng Zhan 鄧展
Dian Lun 典論
Ge Hong 葛洪

hao 號
kongsho ru bairen 空手入白刃
koujue 口訣
Luofu Shan 羅孚山
mifa 秘法
qichi zhang 七尺仗
Sancai Tuhui 三才圖繪
Siyi zuoren 四夷左衽
Shoubi 手臂

Shoubo 手博
shuang ji 雙戟
Wei Wendi 魏文帝
Wu 吳
Zhichuan 稚川
zhi wa 擲瓦
zi 字

Notes

[1] It seems plausible that Ge Hong's reference to Cao Pi's postscript to the *Dian Lun* is meant to be a rejoinder to the condescending manner in which citizens of the northern Kingdom of Wei viewed their counterparts, such as Ge Hong, from the southern Kingdom of Wu—barbarians who fastened their garments from the left side.

[2] Deng Zhan is described as good at boxing/grappling (*shoubi*) and use of the five weapons (*wubing/wurong*), listed in the *Li Ji* (*Record of Rites*) as, bow and arrow, lance, spear, pike, and halberd. Also see Green, Vol. 1 (2001: 67).

[3] The Former Han History (77 CE) notes that the military officer, Gan Yanshou, was exceptionally strong and practiced boxing and stone tossing.

[4] The Cefu Yuangui (1013 CE) describes a three-day battle that took place in 582 between Chinese troops and a Turkic Tujue army. The Chinese fended off the Tujue force, but not before losing over 80 percent of their men and, with their weapons reduced, fighting the Tujue off with their bare fists to the point that one could reportedly see the bones in their hands. Chapter 395 cont. p. 4694. Also see Green, Vol. 1 (2001: 67).

Bibliography – English

Green, T. (Ed.) (2001). *Martial arts of the world: An encyclopedia.* 2 Volumes. Santa Barbara, CA: ABC-CLIO.

Knapp, K. Ge Hong [*Internet Encyclopedia of Philosophy*]. An summary of Ge Hong's life and thought. <http://www.iep.utm. edu/g/gehong.htm>

Bibliography – Romanized Chinese

Ban Gu (1936). *Former Han history.* Shanghai: Zhonghua Press.

Chen Feilong (2002). *Baopuzi outer chapters, modern notes and translation.* Taiwan Commercial Press.

Critique of Literature. <http://ef.cdpa.nsysu.edu.tw/ccw/03/dl.htm>

Li Gang. Ge Hong and his humanistic philosophy. <http://www.siwen. org/xxlr1.asp?id=299>

Wang Liqo (1974). *Discussion of Ge Hong.* Taibei: Wunan Press.

Wang Mengou (1997). *Record of rites—Modern notes and translation. Vol. 1.* Taiwan Commercial Press.

Wang Ming (1985). *An explanation of the Baopuzi internal chapters.* Beijing: Zhonghua Press.

Wang Qinruo (1960). *Library of the grand tortoise (1013).* Hong Kong: Zhonghua Press.

· 7 ·

Taijiquan and Daoism:
From Religion to Martial Art
and Martial Art to Religion
by Douglas Wile, Ph.D.

Misty scene over Wudang Mountains. Courtesy of
www.photo2easy.com. Chen-style taiji practice along
West Lake in Hangzhou city. Photograph by Michael DeMarco.

Introduction

The question of taijiquan's origins—and specifically whether they are
Daoist or not—is no mere academic exercise but a major theater in China's
culture wars for nearly a century. A recent mass-market book *Five Hundred
Unsolved Mysteries in China's Cultural History* lists the origins of taijiquan as
one of Chinese history's most contentious cases. In the 1930s, Tang Hao
(1897-1959), China's first modern martial arts historian, was the target of an
assassination plot for daring to unmask the myth of taiji's Daoist origins, and
in 1999 a prominent martial arts journal, *Jingwu*, after ten years of extensive
coverage, declared a moratorium on the topic. Why all the fuss?

From the middle of the 19th century to the beginning of the 21st, taijiquan has played a very public role in China's cultural life. Exponents of taijiquan were active in the self-strengthening campaigns of the late Qing Reform Movement and Nationalist Revolution; taijiquan played a leading role in the national and provincial martial arts academies of the Republican period; it was standardized and popularized for the masses during the Mao era (1949-1976); and today, taijiquan is still the site of hostile clashes between modernizers and traditionalists, even as it increasingly becomes a leading cultural export and tourist attraction. What began in the 17th century with Huang Zongxi's (1610-1695) wrapping a martial art in religion has come down in the 21st century to Neo-Zhang Sanfeng cultists wrapping religion in a martial art. This chapter will explore the ways in which the construction and deconstruction of a martial arts-Daoist connection has figured in political ideology, cultural identity, and commercial interest during the past century of Chinese history.

Defining taijiquan is at least as controversial as defining Daoism itself. If there are three Daoisms—philosophical, religious, and macrobiotic—there are also three taijis—martial, meditative, and medical. Similarly, there are three stereotypes of taiji masters: recluses who perfect their art with the help of nature or supernatural forces, secret masters living in the world who reveal their art only when pressed or for righteous causes, and public masters who defend the honor of their lineage and accept all challenges. We can trace taijiquan as a philosophy or a lineage, a generic or a brand. All styles claim Daoist philosophical content, and most claim to be successors to a transmission originating with a famous Daoist immortal. The terms "Daoist" and "Confucian" function in Chinese society with roughly the same degree of precision as do liberal and conservative in the West. A Daoist is someone who gathers herbs on misty mountains and meditates in a cave; by contrast, a Confucian sits on a throne or adjudicates stacks of lawsuits. A Daoist seeks seclusion, whereas a Confucian is asked to leave. All the arts and sciences are automatically ceded to Daoism by default because of Confucianism's "amateur ideal" and its distain for instrumental knowledge and individualism. Hence, painting, calligraphy, and poetry are considered Daoist arts; medicine is considered a Daoist science; and even military strategy has a Daoist mystique. The rise of taijiquan represents the attempt to assimilate martial arts into high culture, and for this purpose, only Daoism will do. Methodologically, the history of taijiquan has been told by materialists and idealists. The materialist, or humanist, says that trial and error, or practice, precedes theory, and that knowledge is cumulative, synthetic, and cross-disciplinary; the idealist believes in a transcendent realm of laws or principles accessible only to divine beings or great men. Essentially, the debate in taijiquan historiography has been between creationism and evolution. Of the three kinds of masters in the *Zhuangzi*—sages, craftsmen, and freaks—the creationists side with the sages, the humanists with the craftsmen, and the freaks we will save for the end of our story.

What are the role, status, identity, and image of the martial artist in traditional Chinese society? Body guards, bandits, family feudists, militiamen, assassins, knights-errant, rebels, opera singers, and market place performers. The army had no use for martial artists, either because their skills were flowery and impractical, or because solo virtuosos did not function well in battlefield formation. The subordination of military to civilian authority in politics and the elevation of the civil (*wen*) and military (*wu*) to virtual cosmological categories has allowed the scholar to maintain superiority over the warrior.

The best known association of martial arts with religion in China is the Shaolin monks. As early as the Northern Wei (220-265), they had alternately been persecuted for participating in rebellions but at other times were enlisted by emperors to put down rebellion, piracy, and invasion. Martial arts were most likely to be officially banned during foreign dynasties, such as Mongol and Manchu, and martial arts training, together with quasi-religious doctrines and rituals, were often part of the lure and threat of secret societies. Martial dance for religious ritual and pure esthetics goes back to our earliest written records in China, but the marriage of qigong energetics with a martial art is not attested in detail until Chang Naizhou in the 18th century, a development that reaches its peak with taijiquan in the 19th and 20th centuries.

Whether we define Daoism as an institution with card-carrying members or a certain band on a perennial philosophical spectrum, there is no escaping the heroic efforts to associate or disassociate taijiquan with Daoism. Chinese thinking is often characterized as "correlative" to distinguish it from Western notions of linear causality. Analyzing states and changes based on yin and yang, the five phases, and stems and branches is indeed one mode of Chinese thinking. However, when direct causality is employed, say to assert that the immortal Zhang Sanfeng created taijiquan, we must decide whether this is ignorance, deception, or a discursive practice that places the Wudang Mountains, Zhang Sanfeng, the Internal School, Laozi, the *Yijing*, and taijiquan in a single narrative for the same reason that traditional medicine includes the kidney, "gate of life," foot *shao-yin* channel, ears, brain, hair, nails, anus, the color black, water, and winter, in the "kidney orb." Is it religious faith, the mythic mind, or simply another kind of rational thought? Is building up layer upon layer of Daoist associations for this martial art a form of magical protection against predatory appropriation? This chapter will explore both the ways in which taijiquan partakes of Daoist theory and the efforts to align taijiquan with Daoism. The continued outpouring of fictional accounts of taiji history in the 21st century may appear to be transparently political or commercial, but sometimes it can only be explained as the persistence of a cultural practice that refuses to conform to modern notions of "fact" and the search for a Chinese style of spirituality that retains faith in psychosomatic self-perfection and the possibility of embodied immortality.

Illustration of Zhang Sanfeng taken from the *Collected Works of Zhang Sanfeng* (1844). Illustration courtesy of Douglas Wile.

Zhang Sanfeng and the Internal School

In the 1650s, after years of resistance to Manchu consolidation in the South, philosopher Huang Zongxi (1610-1695) gave up armed struggle and retired to his native Yuyao in Zhejiang Province, where he undertook a comprehensive reassessment of the philosophical and political roots of China's weakness. Among his prolific writings is the *Epitaph for Wang Zhengnan*, written for a former comrade-in-arms, whom Huang praises as a great martial artist, fierce patriot, and righteous knight-errant. He describes Wang as the only living successor to a martial arts lineage called the Internal School (*neijia*) and names Zhang Sanfeng as its founder. He locates Zhang in the Song dynasty, calls him a "Daoist alchemist," and says that Zhang invented the art by reversing Shaolin's reliance on hardness and emphasizing the defensive and offensive advantages of softness.

Huang Zongxi's son, Huang Baijia, himself a student of Wang Zhengnan, wrote a manual of the Internal School art, attributing Zhang Sanfeng's inspiration to a visitation by Xuanwu (God of War) in a dream. As set forth in Baijia's *Internal School's Boxing Methods*, the form bears little resemblance to taijiquan as we know it, contains no reference to internal training, and apart from its soft-style strategy is chiefly distinguished by its pressure point techniques. Moreover, Baijia says that as Wang's only student, the transmission will die with him. The reader is left to ponder whether the Huangs uncritically recorded Wang's account of the Internal School's origins or used biography to encrypt a political allegory for China's survival strategy under Manchu rule.

Contradictions abound: Huang Zongxi was one of the most sober rationalists in Chinese intellectual history and not given to myth making; he was personally opposed to alchemy and the self-delusion of immortality; there is no record of a "Zhang Sanfeng" in the Song dynasty (960-1279); and there is no mention in the Ming (1368-1644) histories or hagiographies of Zhang Sanfeng of any connection between the immortal and the martial arts, just as there are none between Bodhidharma and Shaolin gongfu in the Buddhist literature. The 19th century *Complete Works of Zhang Sanfeng* and 20th century *Zhang Sanfeng's Secret Transmissions on Taiji Elixir Cultivation* do not contain a single credible text, let alone one on martial arts. In other words, Zhang Sanfeng, the immortal martial artist and his Internal School, appear out of nowhere in the Huangs' *Epitath for Wang Zhengnan* and *Internal School's Boxing Methods* and disappear without a trace until the turn of the 20th century, when the first generation of mass market taiji publications begin to name Zhang Sanfeng as the father of taijiquan and the Internal School of Wudang as its precursor.

Drawing of Huang Zongxi dated 1873.

Illustration of Wudang from *Dayue*
Taiheshan Gazetteer dated 1922.

Lineage and Legitimacy

Lineage has been an important means of establishing political legitimacy in China from at least the time of the Shang aristocracy, and it is no less important in the arts. In the Asian martial arts, status devolves from style founder to sons of style founders to "indoor students" of style founders or their sons, and finally to public students, ranked by successive removes. The most prestigious credentials in taijiquan are personal study with members of the Chen, Yang, Wu/Hao, Wu, or Sun families. More esoteric transmissions, usually claiming Daoist origins, are traced from master to disciple, without resort to kinship ties. Lineage establishes personal credentials, but styles often invoke historical, semi-historical, or supernatural founders as totemistic figureheads for the transmission as a whole. Perhaps the only exception in the taiji world is the Chen family, who have simply mythologized their own genealogy. Rather than be left out in the cold, most styles have followed the Yang family lead and adopted Zhang Sanfeng as the patron saint of taijiquan. In keeping with the hard-soft taxonomy established by the Huangs, the terms "Wudang" and "Internal School" became generic designations for martial arts based on

98

yielding and qi cultivation, thus allowing xingyi and bagua to be grafted onto the Internal School tree as sharing the same principles, though lacking a direct line to a Daoist immortal. Where the seams begin to show is in the inconsistency of legendary narratives and in the splicing of the legendary onto the historical period.

For the sake of convenience, and to some degree coherence, let us trace the fathering of taijiquan onto a Daoist lineage through the various styles, style founders, and authors. The first published work introducing taijiquan to the world was Sun Lutang's (1861-1932) 1919 *The Study of Taijiquan*. Sun, student of Hao Weizhen (1842-1920) and founder of the Sun style, credits Zhang Sanfeng as the founder of taijiquan but gives no biographical details. He weaves the various creation myths of three martial arts into a chronology, starting with Bodhidharma and Shaolin, followed by Yue Fei and xingyi, and culminating with Zhang Sanfeng "of the Yuan" with taijiquan. Omitting bagua from his narrative, he specifies that Zhang created taiji as a corrective to the harmful hard-style exercises practiced by his fellow immortality seekers. Although the Sun style continues to be practiced, there are no other major books in this transmission. Hao Weizhen's teacher Li Yiyu (1832-1892) says in his *Short Introduction to Taijiquan* that, "the origins of the art are unknown" (Gu, 1982: 376), and since the Zhang Sanfeng of the *Epitath for Wang Zhengnan* is Song, the source of Sun's attribution seems to be some vague body of martial arts lore. Moving from the mythic to the legendary to the historical, he names Wang Zongyue as author of the classics and Wu Yuxiang (1812-1880) as the link to Chen Qingping (1795-1868) in Zhaobao. This geneology is remarkable for completely leaving Chen Changxing (1771-1853) and Yang Luchan (1799-1871) out of the picture. In fact, the Yang transmission, by far the most influential in the development and dissemination of the art in the last century, is never mentioned.

The second book of the modern era is Xu Yusheng's (1879-1945) 1921 *Illustrated Introduction to the Taijiquan Form*. Xu presents a two part genealogy, tracing the theoretical origins to Fuxi, Yu, the Yellow Emperor, and Hua Tuo, and the practical martial applications to a series of obscure and largely unattested figures, beginning with Xu Xuanping of the Tang, and including Li Daoshan, Cheng Lingxi, Hu Jingzi, and Song Zhongshu. The second phase begins with Zhang Sanfeng, a name which Xu concedes is shared by more than ten figures, none of whom are recorded to have studied martial arts. Xu also gives an alternative version of Zhang's career, making him a Song figure, who single-handedly kills 500 Khitan invaders and transmits his art to hundreds of disciples in Shaanxi. Continuing, he says that during the Yuan, Wang Zongyue revived Zhang's transmission and wrote the classics. Later it was transmitted to Eastern Zhejiang, then to Zhang Songxi and Ningbo, where it was learned by Wang Zhengnan. After many more years it reached early Qing anti-Manchu rebel and folklore hero Gan Fengchi. This is the southern branch. The northern branch continued from Wang Zongyue to Jiang Fa to Chen Changxing and then Yang Luchan. Xu cites the *Prefectural Gazeteer of Ningbo* and *Lost Tales of Knight-Errantry* as his sources, but was also clearly influenced by Song Shuming's early *Republican Treatise on the Origins and Branches of Taijiquan* (Dong, 1948: 108; Wu Zhiqing, n.d.: 268-271). He calls Zhang a "Confucian" and makes no special attempt to hang a Daoist label on his lineage. Xu was an unaligned martial arts promoter, who did not name his personal teachers in the book but acknowledges the consultation of Yang Shaohou and Wu Jianquan at the Beijing Physical Education Research Institute that he headed. The book has no pretensions to critical scholarship, but Xu's work is unique in citing sources for his historical account and in offering multiple versions of taiji's origins. Although Xu's *Illustrated Introduction to the Taijiquan Form* created the formal template for future taiji instructional manuals, this aspect had no imitators.

Sun and Xu established the two prototypical origin myths that came to be adopted by virtually all subsequent writers: Zhang Sanfeng as sole creator of taijiquan, or Zhang as transmitter of an art with earlier antecedents. Exceptions are the Chen family, who had much to lose by myth and everything to gain by keeping creation under their own roof, and the Hao family, representing the Wu Yuxiang style, who did not produce their first book until 1963. The remaining and most prolific styles and writers hail from the Yang and Wu family transmissions. The first publication written on behalf of the Yang family art is that of Yang Chengfu's (1883-1936) student Chen Weiming, who in 1925 published the *Art of Taijiquan*. His very first chapter consists of a fanciful biography of Zhang Sanfeng, complete with all the standard miraculous flourishes. The text makes no reference to martial arts, except for the last sentence, which says that what is known as taijiquan began with him. His second chapter gives a general survey of the evolution of the martial arts, again naming Zhang Sanfeng as founder of the Internal School. Rather than confusing Wang Zong of the *Epitaph for Wang Zhengnan* with Wang Zongyue, however, it simply places Wang Zong a century after Zhang, but in direct line of transmission, and places Wang Zongyue in the Qing as author of the classics and teacher of Chen Changxing. He makes no special pleading for Daoism, but the last chapter consists of a series of quotations from the Laozi, together with parallel principles in the taiji classics. The next book in the Yang transmission is third generation Chengfu's 1931 *Self-defense Applications of Taijiquan*. Probably ghost-written by Dong Yingjie, it begins with a photo gallery of Chengfu and chief disciples and a detailed genealogy from Zhang Sanfeng to Wang Zongyue. He mentions an "Eastern Branch" in Zhejiang, which "regrettably has died out," probably following Baijia's statement that Wang Zhengnan had no successors. However the Henan Branch continues with the Chen's and Yang's. This is followed by a hagiography of the immortal Zhang, and at the end of the book a highly romantic tale of Zhang's cultivation practices. In a fantastic episode, Zhang Sanfeng is lead by a display of heavenly lights to a mysterious cave deep in the mountains. Here he encounters two golden snakes and the source of the celestial emanations: two miraculous spears. Nearby he also discovers a manual called the *Taiji Sticky Thirteen Spear* from whose principles he distills the techniques and sparring form reproduced in the *Self-defense Applications of Taijiquan*. This is perhaps the first example of the genre of pure martial arts fantasy, lacking any antecedents in the Huangs' writings or *History of the Ming* biography of Zhang Sanfeng, to be found in a taiji publication. Chengfu's 1934 *Complete Principles and Practices of Taijiquan*, probably ghost-written by Zheng Manqing, shows a bit more restraint. It contains no genealogy chart, but cites Zhang Sanfeng several times in the prefatory matter as creator of the art. Its narrative genealogy makes no distinction between northern, southern, or eastern branches, and streamlining the transmission, follows Xu Yusheng's introduction of Jiang Fa to deliver the art to Changxing. Departing from Chen Weiming, however, it does not place Changxing and Jiang Fa in a master-disciple relationship. It has no special pleading for Daoism as such.

Yang Chengfu (1883-1936).

Writing in their own names, Zheng Manqing's 1946 (published 1952) *Thirteen Chapters on Taijiquan* contains no genealogy chart, no biography of Zhang, and only two passing references to Zhang as the creator of the Internal School of Wudang, whereas fellow Chengfu disciple Dong Yingjie's 1948 *Principles of Taijiquan* contains not only genealogy chart and biography of Zhang, but reproduces Song Shuming's *Treatise on the Origins and Branches of Taijiquan*, with Dong's personal endorsement of the view that taijiquan predated Sanfeng under different names. Three decades later, undoubtedly provoked by Cultural Revolution anti-feudalism, Zheng felt obliged to defend taiji's lineage against modern-minded scholars in his *New Method of Self-Study in Taijiquan*: "Some people have indulged in wild slander, claiming that taijiquan was not created by the immortal Zhang Sanfeng. I do not know what their motives are." He goes on to recite a number of principles from the *Laozi* shared by taijiquan, concluding, "Who but Sanfeng could have attained this.... Sanfeng took the principles of the Yellow Emperor and Laozi and applied them to the martial arts. Therefore, we call it the internal system. The Buddha was from India, that is, from a foreign country. Bodhidharma was a Buddhist and, therefore, his art is called external" (Zheng, n.d.: 20). Although accepting folklore as fact cannot endear him to historians, nevertheless, Zheng's message as a cultural ideologue is unmistakable: taijiquan's status as the Chinese martial art is inseparable from its special relationship with Daoism. Passing these genes to the next generation, Zheng's Chongqing era student Zhang Qixian in his 1969 *The Essential Principles and Practice of Taijiquan* gives a highly imaginative account of Zhang Sanfeng, complete with precise birth information (nineth day, fourth month, 1247 CE, following mother, nee Lin's, dream of a great stork coming from the sea). According to Zhang Qixian, Sanfeng created the art from observation of a snake's successful defense against a bird, *Yijing* cosmology, and the methods of past martial artists such as Xu Xuanping. Zheng Manqing's Taiwan era student Song Zhijian in his 1970 five hundred page magnum opus *The Study of Taijiquan*, not only accepts the Song Shuming genealogy, but offers complete biographies of all its unattested figures, and even a biography of Song Shuming himself. The trend among Yang lineage authors to magnify the mythological and Daoist trappings over time may be a deliberate counter-discourse to modernist movements on the mainland, but also thumbs its nose at deconstructionist practices in progressive Western scholarship. The scientific backgrounds of many of these authors and the amount of space devoted to legitimizing the art through appeal to Western science is also in stark contrast to their willingness to recapitulate and even embellish the most fabulous origination myths.

The next most widely practiced style is that founded by Wu Jianquan (1870-1942), whose father Quanyu (1834-1902) was a student of second generation Yang family scion, Yang Banhou (1837-1892). As with the Yang transmission, the first published book was by a non-family member, in this case Wu Tunan's 1928 *Taijiquan*, which following on his 1926 *Brief Introduction to Chinese Martial Arts* presents formal biographies of all the unattested figures in Song Shuming's genealogy. Wu's background as an archeologist did not prevent him from exceeding all others in fabricating the minutiae of Zhang's travels and contacts, but there is no mention of how he came by martial skills. Zhang Sanfeng's life is a caricature of the Daoist immortal, but there is no special pleading for Daoism itself. Contradicting the *Epitath for Wang Zhengnan*, he places Wang Zongyue next in line after Zhang and makes Gan Fengchi the end of the southern branch. Jiang Fa of the northern branch brings the art to Chen Village. In his 1984 *Studies on Taijiquan*, Wu, nearing centenarian status, reaffirms his faith in the Xu Xuanping origination myth. In 1935, two other Wu Jianquan students, Ma Yueliang and Chen Zhenmin, published a manual with photos of Wu Jianquan, entitled *Wu Style Taijiquan*. This work takes an unusual approach to lineage. Truncating the Wu Tunan chart, it eliminates the southern branch and all pre-Zhang figures. Moreover, using an evolutionary analysis, it insists that self-defense is a natural ability of man, systematized by Bodhidharma, and refined by Zhang Sanfeng. This Darwinian analysis allows them to simultaneously acknowledge mythological origins, pay homage to the Yang family, and leave room for their own superiority as a further development on Yang. In the same year, Wu Jianquan's second son, Gongzao, published *Commentaries on Taijiquan*, which continues to prune the family tree, eliminating all charts, biographies, and any mention of Zhang Sanfeng. He pays homage only to his own father and close disciples, but this does not mean that he is turning his back on Daoism. On the contrary, he says that taiji's principles, "coincide perfectly with Daoist meditation and really constitute a Daoist practice" (Wu, 1935: 13).

With the phenomenal success of the Yang family in the 20s and 30s, Chen family standard bearer Chen Xin sought to reassert proprietorship of the family art and to buttress in the literary realm what Chen Fake (1887-1957) had accomplished for the family honor in the gymnasia and arenas. To this end, he began in 1919 and published in 1933 the monumental *Introduction to Chen Family Taijiquan*, presenting the Chen family form together with many pages of theoretical essays. By contrast, the traditional Chen family manuscripts discovered by Tang Hao in the village consisted of little more than lists of forms with posture names and a handful of terse training songs. Needing an ancestral progenitor, Chen Xin names Chen Bu, the first to relocate the family from Shanxi to Wen County in Henan, as creator of taijiquan. To compete with the Yang mystique, however, he still needed to establish Daoist credentials. This he accomplished in two ways: first, his book is a tour de force in cosmology and medicine, and second, he introduces a poem attributed to ancestor Chen Wangting in which the latter mentions his devotion to the *Scripture of the Yellow Court*, a famous Daoist cultivation work. He thus attempts to demonstrate, strictly within the parameters of family lineage, that it is possible to create a martial art with Daoist content and inspiration without a Daoist first cause. As we shall see later, rivals in neighboring Zhaobao effectively abandon family lineage and hitch their wagons directly to Zhang Sanfeng.

Positing historical lineages preceded by remote mythological progenitors and ancestors is a common cultural pattern among many peoples. The folkloric process may have been at work with Wang Zhengnan, but it was literati Huang Zongxi and Huang Baijia who presented it to the world. In the case of the Chen's and Yang's, the Chen's had no tradition of Zhang Sanfeng, and Yang Luchan would not have heard this in Chen Village. Even if he had been aware of the *Epitaph for Wang Zhengnan* and *Internal School's Boxing Methods*, unlikely for an illiterate peasant, he probably would not have associated this with the art he was taught in Henan so far from Zhejiang. The Huang documents are the *locus classici* for the Zhang Sanfeng creation myth, and derivative versions were carried in the *Ningbo Prefectural Gazetteer*, *Strange Tales from the Studio of Idleness* and *Complete works of Zhang Sanfeng*. We do not know who made the first link between Zhang Sanfeng and taijiquan, and no two versions are the same, but we do know that the promoters of this lineage were among the educated elite, including many with Western scientific knowledge, and could hardly be considered part of a folk process. Their motivations, then, must have been conscious and deserve further exploration.

The first generation of taijiquan books were written against the background of an unstable republic, warlordism, and the Northern Expedition, but not yet a strong communist movement or imminent Japanese invasion. What is interesting at the present juncture is that in spite of Tang Hao, Xu Zhen, Gu Liuxin and many other's attempts to deconstruct these invented traditions, we now enter the 21st century with claims on behalf of the Yangs more fantastic than anything these pioneering martial arts historians were obliged to explode. Although the first three generations of Yang family masters have been the object of extreme veneration and no small amount of apocrypha, they are still derivative of the Chen art, which in turn is viewed by some as a rustic retention of the exalted art of the immortal Zhang. If Yang Luchan could be linked directly with a Daoist source, this would reduce the Chen role to kindergarten and turn Luchan, whom Tang Hao determined to be a peasant bondservant, into a Daoist initiate.

Daoist monks inside a temple.
Photograph by Kipling Swehla (www.kiplingphoto.com) and
courtesy of the Taoist Restoration Society (www.taoarts.com).

Although Luchan lived in the 19th century and is the founder of taijiquan's most widely disseminated style, there is not a shred of reliable biographical information about him, in fact, while arguably the most famous son of Yongnian County, his name does not appear in the local gazetteer, either as a degree holder, or even as a martial artist. Firsthand impressions of Luchan by grandson Chengfu are seriously undermined by the fact that Chengfu was born twelve years after Luchan's death. Controversies have centered on Luchan's background (was he a peasant or literatus?), his martial arts education (did he learn in Chen Village from boyhood, or did he make the fabled "three pilgrimages?"), and more recently, was he really a tutor to the Manchu princes in Beijing? Questions that might trouble sober scholars have not restrained He Hongming, a student of Li Yaxuan (himself a student of Luchan's grandson

Yang Chengfu), who reports that Li told him that on his "third trip" to Chen Village, Yang was given the "classics" written by Zhang Sanfeng and then set out to the Wudang Mountains to learn inner alchemy from reclusive adepts. This led him to eliminate the jumps, stamps, hard kicks and strikes, and uneven tempo found in the Chen form and to give taijiquan the distinctive "internal" characteristics we now associate with it (He, 1999: 34-35). Zhao Youbin, Lu Dimin, Feng Fuming, and Yong Yangren are also in agreement that Yang Luchan received the classics from Chen Changxing (Zhao, Lu, and Feng, 1989: 22-24; Yong, 89, 26-31). Although this contradicts many firsthand accounts describing the gradual softening of the form through the first three generations of Yang masters and its adaptation to the urban intelligentsia, He Hongming's tale forges a much closer connection between the Yang's and Daoism, making Zhang Sanfeng the author of the taiji classics, putting them into Yang's hands in Chen Village, and sending Luchan himself to the Wudang Mountains to study with "Daoists." This version also minimizes the role of the Chen family and effectively erases the Wu's and Li's. A similar assertion is made in a recent article by Li Shirong, "revealing" that Luchan received the classics from his teacher Chen Changxing, who preserved the Wang Zongyue manuscript of Zhang Sanfeng's writings (Li, 2000: 26-27). Again, this flies in the face of Tang Hao's finding no writings or oral tradition of Zhang Sanfeng in Chen Village and the absence of same in Chen Xin's *Introduction to Chen Family Taijiquan*. While making no attempt to refute, or even acknowledge, the findings of responsible scholars, He and Li seem willing to trade in Yang Luchan's historical role as a humble but gifted lineage founder for an invented role in the Zhang Sanfeng transmission and a Daoist initiate.

A few scholars have managed to avoid being kidnapped in either the Wudang Mountains or Chen Village. Bian Renjie (Bian, 1936: 5-9), Hu Puan (Wu, n.d.: 194), and Zhuang Shen (Zeng, 1960: 223-228) review the many mutually contradictory claims, concluding that the evidence advanced by partisans on all sides is false and credible records still unavailable. Wu Zhiqing, a 1917 student of Yang Chengfu, is able to steer clear of sectarianism and mystification, coming to the enlightened and elegant conclusion that:

> Taijiquan is not a mysterious and bizarre magical art; neither is it
> the shallow skill of body guards and street performers. Rather, it
> is a natural self-defense, exercise, and health system that arises
> from the natural world.   – Wu, n.d.: 1

Similarly, Zhao Ximin (Zhao, 1979: 85-105), Wang Juexin (Wang, 1976: 5), and Zhou Jiannan (Zhou, 1976: 77-99), writing in Taiwan in the wake of the mainland's Cultural Revolution, nevertheless were able to free themselves from Cold War bias to mete out praise and blame on strictly scholarly criteria. However, their writings were not available in mainland China, where they could have served to correct some of the blind spots in Tang Hao's official view, and they were likewise ignored by overseas anticommunist cultural conservatives, just as they are today by the Neo-Zhang Sanfeng taiji religionists. In the end, these voices of reason were not able to carry the day, and one set of narrow views prevailed as the official version on the mainland, while the other became the self-appointed opposition and exclusive export model.

Zheng Manqing lectured on taijiquan, traditional
Chinese medicine, and Chinese philosophy.
Photo courtesy of Kenneth Van Sickle. www.sinobarr.com

Consonance with Daoist Philosophy

Fabricating a lineage from a famous immortal in Chinese folklore is one approach to linking taijiquan to Daoism, but taiji's claim to being the thinking man's martial art rests more securely on its theoretical consonance with Daoist philosophy. Ironically, although the "taiji classics" have many embedded quotations from the *Yijing*, *Great Learning*, *Book of History*, *Records of the Grand Historian*, Zhu Xi, Zhou Dunyi, and Mencius, there are none from the *Laozi* and *Zhuangzi*. The first generation of modern taiji books, those of Sun

Lutang, Chen Weiming, Xu Yushseng, and Chen Xin, are similarly eclectic in their use of philosophical sources. Sun Lutang credits the *Yijing* with inspiring Zhang to soften the qigong regimen of immortality seekers, and though he himself does not cite the *Laozi* directly, the Wu Xingu and Chen Zengze prefaces are devoted chiefly to establishing the Daoist connection. Xu Yusheng says that, "Zhang Sanfeng based his art on the *Confucian* [author ital.] principle of taiji" (Xu, 1921: 2) and mentions Zhuangzi's "from skill we approach the Dao," but makes no special appeal to Daoism as taiji's official philosophy. In fact, in a preface to Xu's work, Yang Chang says despairingly, "In the midst of the current difficulties, most of our educated men escape into Buddhism and Daoism" (Xu, 1921: 4). In Zhang Yiling's preface to Xu's book, he credits Japan's victory over Russia to the former's promotion of judo, which he hastens to point out is borrowed from China (Xu, 1921: 1). Like everyone else, Xu uses *Yijing* cosmology to explain the principles of taijiquan, but says, "Today, science has reached an advanced stage, where it can be anticipated that in the future, geometry and mechanics will be used to explain the principles of taijiquan, without resorting to the *Yijing*" (Xu, 1921; 3). Xu then proceeds to a detailed exposition of Zhou Dunyi and Shao Yong's *Yijing*-based cosmologies and how they relate to taiji.

Representing the Wu Jianquan transmission, Wu Tunan's 1928 *Taijiquan* adopts the Song Shuming genealogy but uses no cosmological language or references to any philosophical school. Instead it praises taijiquan as scientifically superior to both hard Chinese styles and Western calisthenics. Similarly, Chen Zhenmin and Ma Yueliang's *Wu* [Jianquan] *Style Taijiquan* says, "Because taijiquan appears relatively late and its history is fairly short, its system is more clearly delineated.... In all branches of learning or skill, later creations are superior to earlier...and martial arts are no exception to this rule" (Chen and Ma, 1935: 1, 3). This work also emphasizes taiji's consonance with modern science, downplaying cosmological language and debts to traditional philosophy. Representing the Yang transmission, Chen Weiming is sparing with cosmological jargon, but concludes his *The Art of Taijiquan* with a lengthy series of parallel quotations from the *Laozi* and the taiji classics. Fellow Yang Chengfu disciple Dong Yingjie provides a biography of Zhang, but no separate section of parallel quotations. Zheng Manqing, another Chengfu disciple, in his *New Method of Self-study in Taijiquan* gives no biography but provides relevant quotations from the *Yijing*, *Laozi*, and *Neijing*. Yang Chengfu's 1931 *Taijiquan shiyong fa* begins with a biography of Zhang Sanfeng, but has no extended cosmological expositions. His 1934

Taijiquan tiyong quanshu, however, does contain an introductory discussion on philosophical roots, and in Zheng Manqing's preface to the work, he specifically addresses the question of philosophical affinity, giving explicit priority to Daoism. Reviewing other traditional texts that countenance hardness as the natural complement of softness, Zheng finds in *Laozi* the only consistently soft-sided philosophy:

> Only the greatest hardness can overcome the greatest softness; only the greatest softness can overcome the greatest hardness. The *Yijing* says, "Hard and soft rub against each other, and the eight trigrams knock together." The *Book of History* says, "The thoughtful and imperturbable conquer by hardness; the wise and skillful conquer by softness." The *Book of Odes* says, "He would not eat the hard or spit out the soft." But when it comes to the application of hard and soft, there cannot be two approaches. Why is it that Laozi alone says, "The highest softness overcomes the highest hardness," and also, "The soft and weak triumph over the hard and strong?"
>
> – Yang, 1934: 3

For Zheng, the principle of uncompromising softness goes beyond self-cultivation and self-defense, and in national policy constitutes "the means for strengthening the nation and alleviating the people's suffering" (Yang, 1934: 4). Zheng expresses taiji's relationship with Daoism in this simple equation: "Taijiquan enables us to reach the stage of undifferentiated pure yang, which is exactly the same as Laozi's 'concentrating the qi and developing softness'" (Zheng, 1952: 6). In order to achieve this level, however, Zheng struggles with the line in the taiji classics, "Those with qi have no strength." Parsing the distinction between strength, qi, and mind, Zheng combines Laozi's "Concentrate the qi and develop softness" with the inner elixir formula, "Refine the essence into qi and the qi into spirit" to explicate the classics' "The mind must be on the spirit and not on the qi; if it is on the qi, there will be blocks, and where there is qi, there is no strength; without qi there is pure hardness" (Zheng, 1952: 8). It is clear that Zheng looks to Laozi for the highest expression of spiritual attainment and that practice without enlightenment and faith in softness can never lead to "essential hardness" (*chungang*) or "spiritual power" (*shenli*). Zheng's student Song Jianzhi continues this theme, "We cannot be certain who first created taijiquan, but judging from its name and principles, there is no doubt it was a Daoist…Daoism begins with Laozi… and his principles are precisely those governing the practice of stillness and action in taijiquan as well as inner elixir cultivation" (Song, 1959: 11). For Zheng and his disciples, the efficacy of softness could only be demonstrated after a considerable period of "*xue chikui*" (investing in loss), as only "supreme softness" will cause hardness to defeat itself.

It would be difficult to find any martial arts style during the late Qing-early Republican period that did not use Daoist language to legitimize itself, appeal to intellectuals, and contribute to the construction of national identity. It goes without saying that taijiquan shares its movement principles and inner energetics with sister arts xingyi and bagua, but soft-style philosophy was adopted even by Shaolin during this period. The *Traditional Shaolin and Secret Transmissions of Shaolin Boxing*, judged by Tang Hao to be no earlier than late Qing, express Shaolin's principles in terms of hard and soft, full and empty, and the pseudonymous author consistently refers to Shaolin as "the art of softness" (Zunwozhai, n.d.: 1-2; Tang, 1986: 70). In order to further elide any essential philosophical distinction between Shaolin and Wudang, the Traditional Shaolin insists that the terms "internal and external," refer not to training or tactics, but to Shaolin's Buddhist origins. Tang Hao, who studied in Japan, also points out that the language of the Shaolin manuals sounds reminiscent of Japanese judo literature. Thus, at a time when China was under siege by Japan, China's martial arts ideologues may well have been aware of the role of judo in Japan's martial arts revival and in building a sense of superiority to the West and thus adopted its soft-style stance. In fact, the *Secrets of Shaolin Boxing* even attempts to adopt Zhang Sanfeng himself, characterizing him as a Shaolin master who in his later years systematized the "72 pressure point techniques," which he learned from a Daoist named Feng Yiyuan (Zunwozhai, n.d.; 108; Tang, 1986: 79).

No martial art has expended as much effort to establish its philosophical pedigree as taijiquan. The persistence of this view can be seen in a recent article by Ma Yuannian, entitled "Taijiquan and Confucian Thought" ("Taijiquan he rujia sixiang"):

It is well-known that taijquan is a Daoist art and that its symbol is the taiji diagram.... However, historically Daoism, Buddhism, and Confucianism have influenced and learned from each other, and therefore, although purely a product of Daoism, taijiquan has also absorbed some Buddhist and Confucian elements, especially Confucianism's philosophy of the "golden mean."

– Ma, 1998: 32-33

Even in an article ostensibly devoted to exploring the Confucian contribution to taijiquan's development, the author has already conceded that taiji is a "Daoist art."

In the *Laozi*, softness overcoming hardness, or softness within hardness, are presented both as martial ethic and strategy. However, pacifist themes in the *Laozi*, such as, "Compassion allows us to be courageous," and "Weapon are not auspicious instruments," are not nearly as well developed in the taiji literature as in judo, aikido, or even Shaolin. Strategically, the *Laozi's*, "I do not dare to play the host, but play the guest. I would rather retreat a yard than advance a foot," "Courage in daring gets us killed; courage in not killing allows us to live," and "The sage does not contend, and therefore no one in the world can contend with him" become in taiji a defensive strategy of disarming the opponent by apparent yielding, while giving him enough rope to hang himself. Laozi's "nonaction" (*wuwei*) functions in taiji as letting others strike the first blow, neutralizing the incoming energy, sticking to it, borrowing it, and returning it. "Egolessness" (*wuwo*) in the *Laozi* corresponds to taiji's "emptying," so that the opponent's force "lands on nothing." Martial arts writers from Huang Zongxi and Huang Baijia to the present have appreciated the wider allegorical significance of martial arts' soft-style strategy. In a postscript to a 1980 reprint of Wu Gongzao's *Commentaries on Taijiquan* no less a figure than Jin Yong, China's most celebrated martial arts novelist, makes very explicit the relationship between taijiquan, Daoism, and international political strategy:

> Humility invites advantage; pride courts disaster—this is China's political and personal philosophy.... Legend has it that taijiquan was created by Zhang Sanfeng, and Zhang Sanfeng was a Daoist. Taijiquan perfectly expresses Daoist philosophy. However, Daoist philosophy does not advocate pure passivity. Rather, Laozi emphasized that if you want to get something, you must first give something, and thus he said, "Great nations remain humble," meaning that the powerful do not puff themselves up but conserve their strength, while their enemies exhaust themselves. This is the time to strike. — Wu, 1980: 135-37

It is important to remember that in all three of the dominant versions of the Zhang Sanfeng myth, he is not a Daoist quietist but a warrior who goes forth to slay bandits. In Chinese, of course, "bandits" (*fei, zei, kou*) can refer to domestic rebels or foreign invaders. What did "Daoism" mean to turn of the century martial arts ideologues? In the late 19th century, reformer Tan

Sitong strove mightily to harmonize Confucianism, Buddhism, and Christianity, but banished Daoism as encouraging passivity, Legalism as too repressive, and Neo-Confucianism as too puritanical. The seminal works on taijiquan written during the 1920s and 30s obviously had a different understanding of "Daoism." For them, the philosophy of hardness within softness, as for Huang Zongxi, was consonant with the non-confrontational political policy of appeasement pursued by both the late Qing Manchu regime and early Republican KMT (Kuomintang, 1912-1924).

Hundreds of books and articles have been devoted to establishing that taiji practice derives from the *Yijing*'s principles of hard and soft, full and empty. The majority of these are based not only on the idealistic assumption that theory precedes practice but that the *Yijing* is a Daoist work. Since the time of the *Cantongqi* and *Neijing*, cosmological language has been used to describe the internal energetics of meditation and medicine. Its earliest recorded wholesale application to the martial arts is seen in Chang Naizhou and the taiji classics. Because Confucius is traditionally credited with editing the *Yijing* and because of its importance in Song Neo-Confucianism, even some taiji exponents are prepared to concede its Confucian origins. Others, however, fearing dilution of the Daoist association explain that although Zhou Dunyi, author of the *Taijitu shuo* was not a Daoist himself, he stole the taiji symbol and its theory from a Daoist, usually identified as the immortal Chen Xiyi. However, by far the majority of taiji writers simply adopt the *Yijing* as a Daoist work. In the Chinese popular imagination, anything expressing arcane principles in mysterious symbols is associated with Daoism.

Following the correlative logic of the Daoism-*Yijing*-taijiquan triangle, it becomes increasingly clear that during taiji's maturation period in the 19th and early 20th centuries, to say something was Daoist was simply to say that it was Chinese. Calling it Confucian or Buddhist during the late Qing would not do, as the Manchu rulers had successfully co-opted both. Ironically, it is during times of national emergency that the Confucian theme of service to the state seems to have no rallying power and heterodox faiths promising supernatural power and a vision of the sublime come to the fore. Like these millenarian communities and secret societies, the martial arts movement of the turn of the century was not simply escapist but provided a channel for repressed nationalism, religiosity, and masculinity. The promotion of Daoism in China, wedded to the knight-errant (*xia*) tradition, parallels the resurrection of the samurai spirit for Japan's modern army, whose officers carried swords as symbols of the Japanese soul.

Associating taijiquan with philosophy was intended to make it palatable to the intelligentsia at a time when it was imperative to overcome the "sick man of Asia" syndrome and for effete literati to put aside their distain for physical culture. Most martial artists were not members of the gentry class, however, let alone Confucian or Daoist, and literati like Huang Baijia, Wu Yuxiang, and Zheng Manqing have only studied with and glorified them during periods of national emergency. Although 19th century reformers had pointed out that archery and charioteering were part of the classical Confucian curriculum, they could only sell the martial as an expedient for national salvation and could not turn it into something transcendent. If progressive 19th century reformers rejected Daoism as representing passivity and superstition, a subset of conservative intellectuals intuited that only Daoism could transform the martial arts into a Dao.

Illustration of Zhang Sanfeng taken from the *Collected Works of Zhang Sanfeng* (1844). Illustration courtesy of Douglas Wile.

Taijiquan and Daoist Cultivation

With a Daoist lineage and Daoist principles, taijiquan has its figurehead and its philosophy, but there are many paths to Daoist realization. The story of Zhang Sanfeng deriving the principles of a martial art from observing the battle of a snake and crane is like Fuxi abstracting the trigrams from gazing at heaven and earth. Shen Nong, the God of Agriculture, who "tasted a hundred herbs," and master butcher Pao Ding, whose knife met no resistance and so never dulled, are the prototypes of experimentation and induction, "approaching the Dao through skill." The shamanistic aspect of Daoism may be seen in the immortal Zhang's receiving the martial art in a dream from the god Xuanwu. The deductive approach to the Dao is seen in Zhang's reversal of Shaolin's principle of hardness and speed for softness and stillness. Another path is abstraction, or self-emptying and desirelessness, that allows the background consciousness, which is one with the Dao, to come to the fore. Finally, there is inner alchemy, a process that seeks to transform the body's intrinsic energies and achieve immortality through the triumph of the prenatal over the postnatal and yang over yin. It is the last of these that is chiefly the focus of self-cultivation in taiji theory. Self-cultivation, in turn, tends to be represented in two ways: cultivation as the servant of self-defense, or self-defense as a skill leading to enlightenment or the Dao. In the mythic, idealistic realm of Zhang Sanfeng, enlightenment precedes the creation of the martial art, but in the historical realm of human practice, cultivation leads to mastery of the art, and mastery of the art leads to realization of the Dao.

Sun Lutang (1861-1932).

Zhuangzi scoffed at yogic self-cultivation, as did Ge Hong, although for different reasons, and even *Complete Works of Zhang Sanfeng*'s most frequently cited "*Da dao lun*" (Treatise on the Great Dao) says, "Some aspirants engage in massage and daoyin, breathing exercises, and herbs as methods of self-cultivation. Although these methods can temporarily relieve some illnesses, they cannot confer immortality and are considered laughable by true adepts" (Li, 1844: juan 3). Li Xiyue and his Sichuan circle, who forged the Zhang

Sanfeng canon in the early 19th century, had no thought that this might prove to be an embarrassment to early 21st century revivers of Zhang Sanfeng as the patron saint of taijiquan. In spite of attributing the Internal School to "a Daoist alchemist," there is nothing in the *Art of the Internal School's Boxing Methods* that relates to internal cultivation techniques. The Chen family material, likewise, contains no evidence of qigong importations prior to Chen Xin's early 20th century book. We find it full-blown, however, in Chang Naizhou's 18th century writings:

> The central qi is what the classics on immortality call the source yang or what medicine calls the source qi. Because it dwells in the center of the body, martial artists call it the central qi. This qi is the prenatal true monadal qi. Spiritual cultivation produces the inner elixir; martial cultivation produces the external elixir. However, the inner elixir always depends on the outer elixir, for action and stillness mutually engender each other. Proper cultivation naturally results in forming the ethereal fetus and returning to the primordial state.   – Chang, 1932: 1

Interestingly, although Chang and the taiji classics share many verbatim and parallel passages, there are no traceable lineage links between his art and either Chen Village or Wuyang, the alleged site of the classics' find. In the "Author's Preface" to his 1919 *The Study of Taijiquan*, Sun Lutang is very explicit about taiji's potential for self-cultivation, and in a passage that reads like a Chinese Genesis says:

> At the dawn of the creation of heaven and earth, the original qi circulated freely. With the division and union of action and stillness, all creatures came into being, and this is the post-creation realm of form. The pre-creation original qi was wedded to the post-creation material world, and thus the post-creation substance contains the pre-creation original qi. Man, therefore, is a being who combines both the pre- and post-creation qi. However, once man acquired knowledge and desires, yin and yang were out of balance, and our post-creation qi gradually increased, resulting in the decline of yang and an overabundance of yin. Moreover, we are assailed by the six external qi—wind, cold, heat, dampness, dryness, and fire—and subject to the seven emotions. In this way, the body becomes daily weaker, and myriad illnesses appear. The ancients were concerned about this and experimented with herbs to

eliminate illness, meditated to cultivate the mind, and fearing that movement and stillness would not be balanced, invented the martial arts in order to restore the subtle qi.   – Sun, 1919: 1

Except for the concluding sentence, this passage could be the opening paragraph of any of a thousand tracts on inner elixir meditation, and clearly positions taijiquan as a method for realizing the Dao. Substituting the goal of supreme self-defense for immortality, however, Sun, in his *The True Essence of the Martial Arts* says:

When one's art reaches the level of uniting emptiness with the dao, which is the true mind, it is transformed into the realm of the highest emptiness and highest void. When the mind is empty and without a single object, if suddenly something unexpected happens, even without hearing or seeing it, you can sense and avoid it.   – Sun, 1924: 8

Nearly a century later, Sun Lutang's daughter, Sun Jianyun, echoes this same theme:

One of the reasons why xingyi, bagua, and taiji have flourished during the 20th century is that they allow us to become one with the dao, that is, they are martial arts that are simultaneously Daoist arts.
                                                     – Tong, 1999: 12

Radical new voices today, like Guo Tiefeng, however, are prepared to go beyond mere mystical union with the dao and boldly proclaim:

Taijiquan is one of the paths to Daoist immortality and it gives practitioners an air of spiritual otherworldliness.... Taijiquan originated with Laozi and its goal is the attainment of immortality.   – Guo, 1999: 28

This statement puts taijiquan in the service of a Daoism narrowly defined as the pursuit of immortality and is a throwback to Du Yuanhua, whose 1935 *Orthodox Taijiquan* insists,

This art is a vehicle for cultivating the elixir and gaining longevity. After long practice, it can truly allow us to achieve the state of pure yang, that is, immortality.   – Yan, 1997: 8

Although there are at least four different interpretations of the term "internal art" (*neijia*) in common usage today, taiji is considered "internal" because it works from the inside out, that is, training the qi rather than the muscles, bones, and ligaments and aims at developing intrinsic energy (*jin*) rather than brute strength (*li*). As a self-cultivation method, taijiquan has many things in common with other methods, as well as some unique features. The system almost always includes a form and usually push-hands. Like progressing from sheet music to memorization to improvisation, the form and push-hands are the scales, compositions, and duets of body mechanics, internal energy, and self-defense techniques. Ancillary exercises often include sitting meditation to focus on emptying the mind and opening the microcosmic orbit; standing meditation to raise the *yangqi*, lower the energetic center of gravity, and demonstrate how relaxation and abdominal breathing alter the perception of pain; acupressure massage to develop awareness of points and qi channels; and qigong to experience qi mobilization in repetitive single phrase exercises without the mental burden of memorization; and weapons to train qi extension beyond the body. More advanced work may include moving push-hands, fencing, free sparring, and grappling. Like sexual practices, all of these partnering exercises train coolness under fire and stillness in motion; scripts are left behind, and like dancers losing themselves in the music, one enters the realm of "soaring on the laws of the universe."

The path of natural movement is discovered by relaxing, listening inwardly, and slowing down, all of which takes us out of our conditioned mental and physical habits and allows us to drop into the Dao. The slow tempo, taiji's most distinctive external feature, slows the mind and breath, heightens awareness of gravity, momentum, and centrifugal force, and accelerates the strengthening of the legs. The body is emptied of tension and the mind of discursive thoughts and goals. In meditation, preconceptions stand in the way of enlightenment; in taijiquan, preconceptions cause the body to trip over the mind's intentions and prevent us from "forgetting ourselves and following the opponent." The fusion of body, mind, and breath in a moving meditation creates the perfect balance of excitation and relaxation required for the "flow" experience, and by centering the self in the radical present sets the stage for experiencing rare moments of spontaneity (*ziran*). Alignment creates the structural precondition for relaxation and optimizes the body mechanics for neutralizing or issuing energy, while emptying the body of tension allows the qi to concentrate and circulate. With both consciousness and qi rooted in center (*dantian*), the mind and extremities are relieved of leadership roles and practitioners can enjoy the "no-mind" experience of improvisational spontaneity—effortless, egoless, just so.

Illustration found in the military arts manual by General Qi Jiguang (1507-1587) entitled *Book of Effective Discipline*.

Whether couched in the terms of alchemy, cosmology, mythology, or medicine, all Chinese meditation texts are based on restoring body-mind harmony, or the heart-kidney axis, by focusing the mind in the lower abdomen. The injunction to "sink the qi to the dantian" appears in virtually every text of the Li Yiyu and Yang family redactions of the taiji classics, but nowhere in *Qi Jiguang's Boxing Classic*, Huang Baijia's *Internal School's Boxing Methods*, or the traditional Chen family material. The 18th and 19th centuries mark a turning point, then, in martial arts, when Chang Naizhou's writings and the taiji classics show the absorption of cultivation concepts into martial arts practice. Chen Xin's *Introduction to Chen Family Taijiquan* says, "Maintaining the focus in the center is what the Daoists refer to as gathering the *jing* and concentrating the qi so that the concentrated qi reverts to spirit" (Chen, 1934: 139). Chen and others like Zheng Manqing go further than dantian concentration and apply full microcosmic orbit meditation, based on a continuous circuit of qi circulation up the *du* (governing) and down the *ren* (controlling) channels, to taiji practice. It is only a small step then to bringing the entire channel system into the martial arts, with focus on specific acupuncture points and the use of various macrocosmic orbits to circulate the qi throughout the entire body. Other qigong techniques are enlisted by some taiji practitioners to demonstrate supernormal powers to attack acupuncture points (*dianxue*), withstand blows (*tieyi*), protect the genitals (*macangshen*), or issue energy through space (*lingkong faqi*). For taijiquan, and to some degree all the Chinese martial arts, to have adopted the language and methods of qigong and meditation is as natural as the Japanese martial arts borrowing from Zen. Although Western athletes may make use of prayer and psychology, it is the Western dance community that has evinced far greater interest in Indian yoga, Zen meditation, and Asian martial arts.

One of the perennial debates in Daoist meditation, and more broadly in Chinese philosophy, is whether to cultivate the mind (*xing, xin*) first, the body (*ming, shen*) first, or both simultaneously. This discussion is also sometimes framed as stillness (*jing*) versus action (*dong*), or the spiritual (*wen*) versus the martial (*wu*). Exponents of taijiquan have been uniquely well situated to champion the simultaneous cultivation position. Sitting meditators have often held that the *yangqi* sprouting in yin stillness is the pure prenatal yang, but have been criticized by qigong and sexual practitioners as fostering stagnation rather than stillness. Active practitioners, for their part, have sought to generate and mobilize large amounts of qi, but have been criticized for over stimulation and relying on the postnatal. By seeking "stillness in movement and movement in stillness" taijiquan has laid claim to the Golden Mean. This is brought out in a recent article by Feng Zhiqiang:

> Taijiquan is an internal martial art that simultaneously cultivates our intrinsic nature and life. Intrinsic nature and life may be called the heart and kidney…. This dual cultivation through taijiquan allows us to achieve an equilibrium of water and fire and harmony of yin and yang, which promotes the goal of health and longevity.   – Feng, 2000: 18

Dual cultivation may be considered orthodox in Daoist cultivation, but "paired practices" (*shuangxiu*) have been a persistent undercurrent for more than two thousand years. Usually associated with sexual practices, in the wider sense, it also encompasses any form of borrowing or exchanging qi with a partner. The "Yang Family Forty Chapters," attributed to Yang Banhou (1837-1892), contains a unique example of asexual paired practice within a martial arts context. Combining meditation's concept of the mating (*jiao*) of the male/yang consciousness principle with the female/yin physical principle in the body, together with sexual practice's concept of borrowing energy from a partner (*caizhan*) and applying this to martial arts sparring we hear:

> The male body belongs to yin, hence gathering (*cai*) the yin from one's own body or doing battle (*zhan*) with the female in one's own body is not as good as matching yin and yang between two males. This is a faster method of cultivating the body.

In solo meditation, the mind is anchored by the body and the body energized by the mind. In the martial meditation proposed by the Yang family material, the "battle of essences" is played out in the interaction of trigrams and phases represented by the "eight techniques" and "five steps." The text, whose title credits the work to Zhang Sanfeng, uses martial arts in the service of the "Great Learning's" call to "self-cultivation" (*xiushen*) to uncover Wang Yangming's "innate knowledge and ability" (*liangzhi liangneng*) and achieve the state of "sagehood or immortality" (*shengshen*). The technical details are expressed in the language of inner alchemy, and the tone can only be called religious—a martial mysticism promising the warrior the same fruits of self-cultivation as the sage.

Depictions of Chen Taiji postures as seen on a wall in Chen Village.
Illustration courtesy of Stephan Berwick. www.truetaichi.com

Contra Zhang and Officialist History

The same Nationalist government that was prepared to consign traditional Chinese medicine to the dustbin of history and allow Western medicine to win the day tacitly cooperated in the construction of a mythos for taijiquan and created an infrastructure for its dissemination. By the early decades of the 20th century, taiji had its progenitor, its philosophy, its genealogy, a proliferation of styles, a stable of living masters, and an institutional base in the national and regional martial arts academies. As long as writers accepted Daoism as the state religion of taijiquan and Zhang Sanfeng as its chief god, they were free to expand the pantheon or embellish its lore and legends. During the early decades of the Republic (1911-1949) on the mainland, the strongest voices in opposition to this invented tradition came not from hard or other internal styles, but from leftist taiji enthusiasts who resented the art's abduction by conservative ideologues. Thus with a mission to demystify taijiquan and return it to the people, Tang Hao visited Chen Village in the early 1930s, followed by fieldwork in the Wudang Mountains to locate descendants of Zhang Sanfeng and in Ningbo to find traces of the Internal School. He found nothing in the Wudang Mountains or Ningbo, but in Chen Village discovered form manuals that were clearly successors to Qi Jiguan's *Boxing Classic* and precursors to the Yang and subsequent forms. In the *Chen Family Biographies* and *Chen Family Genealogy*, he found entries stating that Chen Wangting, who served as a militia commander in Wen County in 1641 and retired after the fall of the Ming, was the creator of the family form, together with a poem attributed to Wangting saying that he choreographed martial arts forms in his retirement and always kept the *Huangting jing* by his side (Chen, 1933: 477; Tang/Gu, 1963: 7). Tang and collaborator Gu Liuxin acknowledge the Chen debt to Qi's *Boxing Classic*, as seen in the Chen form posture names and the "*Quangjing zongge*" (Poem on the Boxing Classic) but say that Chen's original contribution was the development of push-hands as a unique method of training tactile sensitivity and internal energy in sparring without protective gear. What Tang Hao found in Chen Village, then, was a copy of Qi's *Boxing Classic* and living family members who still practiced one of the several forms recorded in the family manuals; what he did not find were the "classics" or any written or oral tradition regarding Zhang Sanfeng or Wang Zongyue.

In order to close the gap between the Chen family forms and the "classics" theory, Tang asserted that Wang Zongyue, who is credited with writing some of the texts in the Wu/Li and Yang family corpuses, must have studied in Chen village and summarized the principles of soft-style pugilism in these short compositions. Xu Zhen, also a modern-minded contemporary of Tang, could not accept that the Chen family developed taijiquan in isolation and so countered that Wang Zongyue must have been the transmitter who brought the art to Chen village. Having discovered the cradle in Chen village and giving taiji a humanistic genesis, Tang was somewhat credulous in accepting the authenticity of the "bookstall" manuscript he found in Beijing, and whose author, "Mr. Wang of Shanxi," he assumed to be Wang Zongyue, and the Chen family genealogy and biographies written or altered by Chen Xin. During the Mao era (1949-1976), idealistic accounts of human achievements were overturned as feudal dregs, a conspiracy to deprive the people of credit for producing knowledge with their own hands through trail and error. For Tang Hao, then, the prime mover is the masses. Qi Jiguang is a flesh and blood historical figure, and his form is a synthesis of the best features of sixteen popular styles he collected among the people. The Chen family is a flesh and blood grass roots family, and their family form is based on Qi's *Boxing Classic*. There is no need to kidnap a Daoist immortal and turn him into a martial artist and a patriot. Qi's credentials are impeccable: a patriotic general, a military reformer, a student, synthesizer, and standardizer of popular martial arts styles, and the most influential military mind since Sunzi. The changes—softening of the form and the addition of theory—in the transmission from Qi to Chen to Yang can all be explained by evolution.

Tang Hao's views held sway through the fifties, when the torch was passed to Gu Liuxin, who promoted Tang's thesis in a series of books, martial arts dictionaries, and even the *Chinese Encyclopedia*. Successors to Tang, Xu, and Gu still exist, but serious scholarship has been so marginalized by sensational historical fiction that, for example, a prefatory note by the editors of Wuhun to Mo Chaomai's *Study of the Late-Qing Manchu Princes* apologizes for the "dryness" of the article, that uses the *Draft History of the Qing Dynasty* to overturn the long held Yang family legend that Luchan taught taijiquan in the palace and garrison of a Manchu prince (Mo, 1997: 43). Wu Wenhan uses legitimate historical documents, such as *True Record of the Taiping Rebels' Attack on Huaiqing Prefecture)* and *Diary of the Defense of Huaiqing Prefecture* to demonstrate that Chen family accounts of the time and success of Chen led militia in repelling the rebels was exaggerated (Wu, 1995: 17). Yan Han calls for putting aside subjectivity, emotionalism, and sectarianism and a return to Marx's admonition: "Do not be concerned that your research conclusions fail to correspond to your subjective desires or popular theories but only that they reflect objective laws and historical fact" (Yan, 1999: 10). Pan Jianping compares the claims of the Neo-Zhang Sanfengists to the theory of "the divine right of kings" and restates Tang's gradualist approach in these words: "The formation of taijiquan is a synthesis of Ming dynasty martial arts, especially the thirty-two postures of Qi Jiguang's *Boxing Classic*, together with ancient qigong practices, channel theory, and proto-materialist yin-yang and five phases theory" (Pan, 1999: 51).

The pace of retiring errors in received wisdom is proceeding at a far slower rate than new fantasies are being churned out. In a strange convergence of Western orientalism and Chinese self-orientalization, many practitioners East and West would rather believe that they are participating in a practice with divine origins than a "synthesis" analyzed by intellectual historians; they would rather be part of something more romantic than mere human history, and so the voices of rationality grow smaller and smaller in a marketplace where fantasy is the ultimate product. Taiji religionist Li Zhaosheng's assertion that taijiquan cannot sustain itself without Daoist trappings and the promise of immortality takes the experience of the art out of the practitioner's sensorium and locates it in the realm of religion.

Yang Chengfu (1883-1936) in Single Whip posture.

The only expressed opposition to Mainland officialism during the 1950s through the 1970s came from cultural conservatives in Taiwan, Hong Kong, and overseas Chinese communities. The formula of most early 20th century taiji ideologues was patriotism, popularization, science, and mystification. The Communists eliminated only the mystification, using modern scholarship and science to explain taiji's history, theory, and practice. Myth deprived the people of their proud history, and lineage monopolized the knowledge that could benefit the whole nation. The psychosomatic state of relaxation in action induced by taiji practice is not described in terms of spiritual attainment but medicine and psychology. Conservative exponents of taiji believed that taiji's principles were consistent with Western science, but Western science was too crude to explain all of taijiquan. For this, a knowledge of traditional medicine and meditation was necessary. In effect, this amounted to the essentialist position that you had to be Chinese to grasp the secrets of taijiquan. If science and history could explain all of taijiquan, then anyone could master it, and it could no longer function as an ultimate refuge for Chinese identity. The thrust of arguments by cultural conservatives was that Chen Village was too marginal and the Chen family too undistinguished to create something as sublime as taijiquan—it could only have been created by an immortal. In the Chinese language postscript to Huang Wenshan's 1974 *Fundamentals of Tai Chi Chuan*, the author confesses to having been carried away in his youth by May Fourth Movement anti-feudal rhetoric and doubting

Zhang Sanfeng, but after several decades of reflection has shaken off the May Fourth hangover and is coming home to Zhang (Huang, 1974: 515). If he was pushed one way by the May Fourth Movement, it is likely he was pushed the other by the Cultural Revolution. A reverse example is Wang Xinwu, whose 1930s An Exposition of the Principles of Taijiquan followed Song Shuming's fabricated lineage, but in the prefaces to his 1959 mainland and 1962 Hong Kong reprints allows that these tales were merely "myths" (Wang, 1959: n.p.; 1962: 2). Nevertheless, in communist and conservative, we see two different paths to national salvation: give the people faith in divine assistance or give them confidence in their own two hands.

Yang family spokesmen never denied their debt to Chen Village, but at the same time were at pains to construct a supernatural genesis for taijiquan. Chen Xin, for his part, strove to return the honor to his family by doctoring the family records and writing a book displaying encyclopedic mastery of medicine, cosmology, and meditation. Later generations of Chen family exponents obviously were comfortable with the official history of taijiquan and in so doing renounced any future claims to connection with Zhang Sanfeng. In exchange, they were allowed to glory in their ancestors. In the 1980s, Chen Xin's vision of the Chen family taking its rightful place in taiji history has been realized by a generation of Chen family members who have turned the village into a Mecca for training and competition and have made Chen-style taijiquan the fastest growing style on the international circuit. Neighbors and rivals in Zhaobao, however, have taken the opposite tack and have thrown in with the Wudang camp. Thus we can see that Cold War era taiji sectarianism, with divisions primarily along ideological and cultural lines, has given way today to the reemergence of lineage and free markets, with a return to family businesses and the rise of taiji tourism.

The Wudang-Zhaobao Axis

Until the recent Wudang revival, it was impossible for Daoism to reach out to taijiquan. Taiji was a lived practice, officially promoted for health and sport, although stripped of its feudal trappings of lineage, discipleship, and mythology. Daoism, however, which in the popular imagination had meant chiefly exorcists, recluses, talismans, idols, and elixirs, and in the Mao era smashed temples and defrocked priests, had no voice to reach out to taijiquan. Huang Zongxi's Zhang Sanfeng was "an alchemist from the Wudang Mountains" who "slew more than a hundred bandits," thus uniting the wizard and the warrior. The Shaolin monks may have practiced martial arts, but this was by no means typical for Buddhist monks. Our earliest records of shamanism depict exorcists brandishing weapons in a dance-like ritual to drive out demons, but the power here is magical and not technical. Likewise, Daoist immortal Lü Dongbin is pictured as a great swordsman, but this is an operatic caricature, having more to do with the romance of the sword than the fusion of qigong with martial arts. The unleashing of free market forces has now made it possible for the "Wudang" brand, formerly exploited by the Yang's of Hebei, to be brought back to its homeland in Hubei. As a center of Daoist activity, the Wudang Mountains, located in the northwest corner of Hubei Province, reached its peak in the early Ming but gradually declined, nearly disappearing by the late Qing. The Wudang Mountains are traditionally considered the site where Xuanwu (God of War), associated with the seven constellations of the northern sky and with the tortoise and snake, engaged in Daoist practices and attained immortality. He was elevated to the status of a celestial "emperor" (*di*) during the Yongle reign (1402-1424) of the Ming and thus became the logical choice to visit Zhang Sanfeng in a dream.

Illustration of Zhang Sanfeng taken from the *Collected Works of Zhang Sanfeng* (1844). Illustration courtesy of Douglas Wile.

Tang Hao's investigations in Wudang and Ningbo found no successors to Zhang Sanfeng or his Internal School. Recently, however, a number of practitioners have come forward claiming to be just that. It was not until after Mao's death that dissenters to the official view began to surface, and in 1980 the National Martial Arts Exhibition held in Wuhan featured a demonstration by Jin Zitao of a style allegedly preserved in the Wudang Mountains.

Jin was subsequently invited by the Wuhan Physical Education Committee and the Hubei People's Publishing Company to teach in Wuhan and publish a book on the form whose name was shortened to *Wudang taiyi wuxingquan*. Jin moved to Danjiangkou, the nearest city to Wudang, and began to teach there. In 1982, the Wudang Martial Arts Resrearch Association was founded in Danjiangkou, and by 1989 a coalition of Hubei martial arts groups, physical education institutes, research associations, and publishers petitioned the National Physical Education Committee for permission to research the "origins, varieties, and characteristics of Wudang martial arts." As a result, the topic was included as a panel in the academic conferences held in conjunction with planning for China's participation in the 1990 Olympics. They published their findings in a monograph entitled *Studies on Wudang Boxing* in 1992. Their conclusions may be summarized as follows:

1) Zhang Sanfeng was an historical figure;
2) he created a martial art;
3) the martial art he created is unique in its theory and technique;
4) the development of the Wudang School split into many paths, many levels, and many personalities; and
5) the theory that "Zhang Sanfeng did not exist" and that "The Wudang Mountains produced no martial art" is untrue.

Although the authors explain the paucity of credible records as, "Those who have realized the dao conceal their traces," nevertheless, they are prepared to assert that Zhang Sanfeng's birthplace was Yizhou and his dates 1247-1464, arriving at this by the same method that establishes the age of the world by adding the generations since Adam. That the state-run Beijing Physical Education Institute Press would put their imprimatur on a work that unflinchingly announces that Zhang Sanfeng lived 217 years shows how far we have come since the days of scientific socialism. The quality of the evidence marshaled for this study does not justify a claim that Zhang existed, let alone that he lived 217 years, but the study's sins go beyond mere wishful thinking to outright intellectual dishonesty. In Chapter Five, the very first expert witness called in defense of the Zhang Sanfeng theory is none other than Xu Zhen. The editors disingenuously quote from his 1930 *Introduction to Chinese Martial Arts*: "The southern styles of martial arts originated with Zhang Sanfeng of the Wudang Mountains, and of these, taijiquan is the most important." Of all the sources cited in this chapter, Xu alone possesses credentials as a martial arts scholar; however, the authors of the *Studies on Wudang Boxing* commit a serious sin of omission when they fail to mention that Xu completely reversed himself and publicly disavowed the Zhang Sanfeng theory in his more mature 1936 *A Study of the Truth of Taijiquan*:

> The martial arts abound in misrepresentations, but none surpass taijiquan in this regard. Originally, I failed to study the matter carefully and simply followed the view of one school as if it were fact.... The Chen family documents say nothing about Zhang Sanfeng creating taijiquan, and neither do the Wu family writings. In fact, Li Yiyu clearly states that the creator of taijiquan is unknown.... Zhang Sanfeng only appears in the Yang family writings and was clearly added by their followers.
>
> – Deng, 1980: 112

The tactic of quoting from Xu's earlier work was previewed in Wan Laiping and Yan Mei's 1989 *Wudang Taijiquan* (Wan, 1989: 1), published in Hubei under the sponsorship of the Hubei Physical Education Committee, and in fact, Wan's father, the famed Wan Laisheng's 1943 *Introduction to Original Taijiquan* was one of the pioneers in promoting the idea of a transmission independent of the Chens and Yangs. The three research associations who signed onto the publication of the *Studies on Wudang Boxing*, its 29 authors and editors, and the press who published it cannot have been unaware of Xu's retraction. Nevertheless, this is but one example of the egregious dishonesty that characterizes a book that is now the intellectual cornerstone of a commercial empire to capitalize on the Wudang mystique. These include the journal *Wudang* and the Danjiangkou Wudang Martial Arts Research Association, whose training facilities, guest accommodations, art gallery, and public relations center serve to "propagate Wudang culture at home and abroad." Independent origination of other martial arts with well-developed qigong internals is not impossible, as Chang Naizhou's form and writings amply demonstrate, but too many of the new pretenders are simply Yang wine in Yang bottles with antique Daoist labels. The undated early Republican Zhang Sanfeng's *Secret Transmissions on Taiji Elixir Cultivation*, showing a figure in ancient Daoist priest robes performing Yang Chengfu's form is a perfect example.

Jealous of Yang family success, the Chen family has mounted a more than eighty year campaign to gain market share of taiji glory and profits. More recently, neighboring Zhaobao Town has made a bid to enter this market with capital based on the survival of Zhaobao taijiquan, a close cousin of the Chen-style, and the account of taiji history put forward by Du Yuanhua (1869-1938) in his 1935 *Orthodox Taijiquan*. Du was a student of Ren Changchun, who was a student of Chen Qingping (1795-1868). Du traces a transmission that extends all the way from Laozi, whom he credits with creating taijiquan, to contemporary Zhaobao masters. Accounts of Zhang Sanfeng variously place him in the Song, Yuan, or Ming dynasties, but interestingly Du allows only five generations between Laozi and Zhang. Of the immortal Zhang, he says:

> Zhang Sanfeng perfected this martial art to the level of the miraculous and his skill surpassed all others at that time…. His accomplishment in the martial arts is comparable to Confucius' in the realm of letters and sagehood.   – Yan, 1996: 10

According to Du, Zhang's transmission was brought to Zhaobao by Jiang Fa, a shadowy and controversial figure in Chen and Yang folklore. Du paints Jiang as a native of Wenxian County, born in 1574 near Zhaobao, who went to study with Wang Linzhen in Shanxi and returned to found a lineage whose seventh generation master was Chen Qingping, the man whom Wu Yuxiang is said by Li Yiyu to have studied with for a month after his initial introduction to taijiquan by Yang Luchan. Placing Zhaobao in a direct line from Laozi, Zhang Sanfeng, and Jiang Fa effectively invalidates every other version of taiji history and every other lineage or style. Moreover, Zhaobao proponents have recently published a manuscript purported to have been copied in 1918 and containing writings on taijiquan from the first three generations of Jiang Fa's transmission. One of the texts is attributed to Jiang himself and is essentially identical with the *Treatise on Taijiquan* attributed to Zhang Sanfeng in the Yang family redaction of the classics. The rest are original, though whether they are of the vintage and authorship claimed is another matter (Yuan Baoshan, 1996: 3-5). If they are genuinely of the 16th and 17th centuries as claimed, they would be by far the oldest received documents on taijiquan and would supplant the existing "classics," which only exist in Li Yiyu's hand from the late 19th century. Zhaobao promoters point out that Zhaobao Town has been a prosperous commercial crossroads for over 2,500 years, and all of the texts have the name taiji in their titles, but they do not explain why neither the art nor the name were known to Qi Jiguang or Huang Zongxi, or how it dared to violate the imperial name taboo of the first Manchu emperor, Huang Taiji.

128

During the 1930s, national salvation was uppermost in the minds of Chinese intellectuals, and few failed to appreciate that spiritual resources would be as critical as material in determining China's fate. Qi Jiguang had already pronounced martial arts largely irrelevant to mass warfare in the 16th century, how much more so in an era of bombers, submarines, and nerve gas? A shared theme of all the martial arts publications from the 1930s through the 40s is that martial arts, in general, and taijiquan specifically, can promote the health of the nation and kindle a spirit of confidence and resistance. Some, seeing a deeper spiritual vacuum, presented it as a Daoist path to enlightenment. Du says, "The purpose of taijiquan is to cultivate the elixir and to demonstrate to the world that practicing this art can promote longevity, and after long training, allow us to attain pure yang, or immortality" (Yan, 1996: 11). This points out very vividly how far the inner alchemy vision of spirituality through self-deification differs from the Western worship of God or the Confucian worship of ancestors.

Zhang Sanfeng.

Zhang Sanfeng in Our Time

For sheer contentiousness, the Zhang Sanfeng case can only be compared to issues of racism, sexism, abortion, and homosexuality in American culture. At the dawn of the 21st century, the pendulum has once again swung towards the myth-makers. Western practitioners of taijiquan, with their monotheistic, atheistic, or "only begotten son" backgrounds are apt to view Zhang Sanfeng as simply an historical figure with some innocent Daoist embellishments. They are not likely to understand China's culture wars, polytheism, or embodied immortality. As a counterpoint to the dour Confucian scholar, the Chinese folk and artistic imaginations have populated novels, operas, and temples with sword slinging heroes like Sun Wukong, Guan Gong, and Lü Dongbin. Moreover, the custom of attributing the creation of martial arts to figures like Bodhidharma, Yue Fei, and Emperor Taizu of the Song makes it not surprising that Wang Zhengnan credited Zhang Sanfeng with creating the Internal School art.

The construction of the cult of Zhang Sanfeng during the Ming, the naming of Zhang as founder of the Internal School in the early Qing, the revival of the Zhang cult by the Sichuan Sect of Daoism in the mid-19th century, and the crediting of Zhang as creator of taijiquan in the early 20th century have all been noted by historians of Daoism and the martial arts. Now in the 21st century, we can report a renewed push, not simply to reassert Zhang's paternity in the taijiquan realm, but to refurbish his cult and to promote taijiquan as a religious path. What contemporary scholar Huang Zhaohan said in the 1970s and 80s of Qing dynasty Zhang Sanfeng cult promoters Wang Xiling (1664-1724) and Li Xiyue (c. 1796-1850) has proven to be surprisingly prophetic in the 1990s and beyond. In surveying the authenticity of works in the 1844 (reprinted 1906) *Complete Works of Zhang Sanfeng* compiled by Wang Xiling, Huang finds six forgeries, seven self-serving propaganda pieces for Li Xiyue's "Western Sect," and four pieces produced by planchette. He concludes that it would be a mistake to judge them by modern scholarly standards and offers the following perspective:

> Their research methods were uncritical, and they indiscriminately collected all materials whether historical, legendary, apocryphal, or mythological.... Only if later scholars are careful to use these materials critically will they arrive at the correct conclusions.... Regardless of Wang's research methods, they nevertheless show a tremendous expenditure of time and effort.... Because the object of their study was a Daoist and belongs to the category of Daoism, we cannot avoid the judgment that these are religious activities and that they were leading religious lives. – Huang, 1988: 110

This characterization applies perfectly to today's Neo-Zhang Sanfengists: their "research methods" are precisely the same, and their religious discourse every bit as ardent. Modern martial arts historians were once faced only with the task of extricating taijiquan from Zhang Sanfeng and scholars of the history of religion with showing the inauthenticity of the *Complete Works of Zhang Sanfeng*. The Neo-Zhang Sanfengists, however, require us to do both all over again. In his *Summary of Zhang Sanfeng's Inner Elixir Theory*, Yang Hongling plainly states: "As a kind of religious thought, Zhang Sanfeng's Daoist inner elixir theory is the product of social and historical conditions, together with Daoist theory and his own thinking and culture" (Yang, 1997: 28). The critical word here is "religious." Although containing no mention of martial arts, the reproduction of key *Complete Works of Zhang Sanfeng* meditation texts in today's martial arts journals, along with copious annotations, colloquial translations, and biographies of lineage successors fishes for converts to the cult of Zhang Sanfeng in a pool already familiar with his name.

It is obvious that the outpouring of religious sentiment toward Zhang Sanfeng that fills the pages of today's martial arts magazines is part of a broader "roots seeking" and "cultural reflection" movement in China. The basic message of the Zhang cultists is that socialism killed China's soul. One of the most passionate spokesmen for Zhang Sanfeng fundamentalism is Li Zhaosheng, who begins from the premise that Daoism is China's soul:

> Emperor Yingzong of the Song declared the fifteenth day of the second lunar month, Laozi's birthday, to be True Primordial Source Holiday. That is to say, it is only with the birth of Laozi that the Chinese people have a soul. This is the most ancient 'soul of China.'   – Li, 1998: 6

The equation, then, is that Daoism is the soul of China, and taijiquan is the vehicle for its realization. Being a religion, though, health or ethics are not enough: we must have miracles. Therefore, Li Zhaosheng, who proclaims himself an 18th generation successor to the *Xiantian taijiquan* (Primordial taijiquan) style recounts an anecdote of his teacher Cai Xiang: Master Cai was collecting ginseng in the mountains when he spied an heroic figure in flowing robes performing a sword form among the trees. Spellbound, Cai continued to observe him from afar for several days. When he ventured to ask the personage his name, he was told that his surname was Zhang. Later, the figure appeared to him in a dream and revealed his true identity: the immortal Zhang Sanfeng (Li, 1998: 7). A Zhang Sanfeng sighting in the 20th century, reported with absolute credulity on the eve of the 21st is the nicest capsule of post-modernism anyone could ask for. Although Li Zhaosheng himself does not claim to have seen Zhang Sanfeng, it has been his lifelong ambition as an artist and a Zhang devotee to create a worthy iconography for the immortal's veneration. Criticizing previous efforts as either too barbaric or too effete, he proposes to create a portrait combining traditional techniques, the principles of physiognomy, and even the best of Western influences to capture the otherworldly aura of the immortal. Portraiture as an act of piety, according to Li's description, then, has nothing in common with life drawing or photography, but involves seeing with the inner eye of faith.

The Confucian state had always viewed martial artists as trouble-makers, but the Chinese Communists took up the self-strengthening theme of the 1890s and May Fourth Movement, giving state sponsorship to the martial arts as part of a national health and recreation program. In exchange for mass promotion, the martial arts were to give up secrecy and superstition. Nationally standardized and simplified forms replaced family transmissions, and training moved out of courtyards and backrooms into parks and gymnasiums. Though martial arts have joined the free market since the early 1980s, Li Zhaosheng resists any effort to secularize taijiquan, saying:

> Taijiquan, like other arts at that time, was transmitted by alchemists and recluses and later spread among the masses…. A martial art that seeks only to promote health is immature and cannot sustain itself…. "Internally upholding the way of inner alchemy" means that we can sprout feathers and ascend to heaven, attain life everlasting, cure the sick and infirm, and save all living things; "externally showing the point of the weapon" means that we possess the ultimate martial art technique and take killing evil people as our motto…. Those who say that everything is created by the laboring masses seem to be intelligent but on careful examination are not.   — Li, 1998: 6

Li's explicit opposition to the official policy of promoting martial arts for health, and his appeal to restoring them to the traditions of inner alchemy and knight-errantry, is essentially an anti-modernist position. In fact, his standard for historical validity is, "Only the descendants of the lineage are qualified to tell the story of its origins" (Li, 1996: 8). This flies in the face of modern scholarly notions of objectivity and the well-known tendency of styles to exaggerate their own lineages, while imposing an elitist and occultist definition on Daoism. However, at the same time as he champions Zhang Sanfeng as the creator of taijiquan, he denies the origination legends of xingyi and bagua, using opposite arguments. Xingyi, he says, was not created by Yue

Fei, and bagua does not qualify as a true martial art because it cannot point to an immortal creator who preceded historical founder Dong Haichuan. In the end, he goes so far as to say that even taijiquan in its present form does not qualify as "a method for realizing the dao through the martial arts" because it "does not follow the acupuncture channels," as does Li's own style, the *Jouzhuan bapan youlongzhang* (Li, 1996: 9). Li insists that only the superficial aspects of the elixir teachings are made public through the martial arts, just as medicine is but a diluted version of the knowledge held by Daoist adepts and immortals and dispensed out of compassion for the masses. Li is thus willing to sell out taijiquan for the sake of promoting the new cult of Zhang Sanfeng. Fellow cultist Zheng Qing also holds that taijiquan is simply a debased version of a secret Daoist art:

> Taijiquan originally consisted of the external postures of the Daoist's "Taijimen jiugong taijishou," which included standing, sitting, and reclining postures. Because it features the internal principles of movement arising from stillness and advocates training through nonaction, when the qi channels within the body are activated, there is an internal power produced with movement. Practitioners will experience the sensation of a flow of qi that propels the body as it moves. This action is accompanied by a feeling of advancing with circular movements, and thus it is called "taijiquan." However, Zhang Sanfeng of the Ming felt that "Taijimen's" emphasis on non-action and the esoteric nature of the internal training, its secrecy among the five branches of Daoism, together with its requirement of open qi channels, spiritual enlightenment, and long dedication made it difficult for people to understand and accept. Therefore, he eliminated the difficult training and secrecy and presented some of the external postures of "Taijimen jiugong taijishou" to the world.
>
>   – Zheng, 1998: 40

It is difficult to know at this stage whether these efforts to pull taijiquan back into the shadows is a sincere religious impulse or simply cynical brandsmanship in a market that has reverted to family or Daoist lineage as a test of legitimacy rather than physical education diplomas or tournament trophies. Today, anticommunist progressives are still looking West, while anticommunist conservatives are still looking to Daoism. The government seems sensitive to progressive criticism but tolerant of reactionary, as long as it refrains from politics.

Li Zhaosheng's ingenuity as a marketing strategist is truly astonishing. He understands that some of the genies released by the communist government will be very difficult to put back in the lamp: the simplified characters and the Twenty-four Posture Taiji Short Form, for example. Recognizing that tens of millions of people already practice this form, Li has attempted to appropriate it for his own purposes, writing a manual (*pu*) in the archaic seven character rhymed couplet style, with all the old flowery language of inner alchemy, and declaring that its purpose is, "Using the *Yijing* to penetrate the great mystery and realize the dao; using the martial arts to illuminate the True and achieve enlightenment" (Li, 1997: 24). Li has thus not only created a counter-discourse but boldly appropriated the state's productions and recast them in an ancient mould, like dragging pottery in the dirt to create instant antiques. Evidence of fissures in the cult's consensus have already begun to appear, however, as Zhang Jie, who believes that Zhang Sanfeng is the reviver of a still older tradition rather than the creator of taijiquan, is taken to task by Li Shirong and Wu Tierong for weakening the Zhang genesis position and for accepting as authentic the transparently spurious Zhang Sanfeng's *Secret Transmissions on Taiji Elixir Cultivation*. They correctly point out that this counterfeit collection includes a supposedly ancient form that is identical with the Yang form in Chen Weiming's *Taijiquan shu*, and its *Treatise on the Necessity of Cultivating the Spirit and Concentrating the Qi in Practicing Taijiquan* was authored by Wu Tunan and published in his 1931 *Taijiquan* (Li and Wu, 1998: 26-27).

So far we have examined attempts to link taijiquan with Daoism based on bald assertions and simple articles of faith. Another more sophisticated approach, however, deploys pseudo-scholarly methods, riddled with weak links and unwarranted leaps, to defend the paternity of Zhang Sanfeng.

Lu Dimin and Zhao Youbin use textual techniques, teasing out the seven character mnemonic verses embedded in the classics, attributing these to Zhang, and assigning the rest to Wang Zongyue's commentary or Wu Yuxiang's notes (Lu and Zhao, 1992: 7). Li Shirong supports this analysis but is careful to admit that Chen Wangting is indeed the creator of the Chen-style, which he accepts as valid but derivative of the root "Thirteen Postures" transmitted by Zhang Sanfeng. He does not bother to refute the Li Yiyu "Postscript" assertion that the Wu brothers found the classics in a salt shop in Wuyang, Henan, but does insist that Yang received the complete version first, obliging Wu Yuxiang to copy some portions from Yang (Li, 2000: 10-13). Teasing classic from commentary is a standard scholarly procedure, but it cannot turn Zhang and Wang into bona fide historical figures or prevent Wu Yuxiang and Li Yiyu from writing the "classics" themselves, as some scholars have proposed.

Chen Weiming (1881-1958).

In a 1999 article, Li Shirong, again attempting to appropriate the enemy's rhetoric, characterizes his own scholarly method, saying: "Its logic is consistent with dialectical materialism" (Le, 1999:6). Using this method he correctly challenges Tang Hao's assumption that the "Master Wang of Shanxi who lived during the Qianlong reign of the Qing" and authored the *Yinfu Spear Manual* is the same as Wang Zongyue. However, the basis for his skepticism is not the high probability that the *Yinfu Spear Manual* and accompanying biography found by Tang in the Beijing bookstalls is a forgery, but because to accept it would be to deny that Zhang Sanfeng and Wang Zongyue were both Ming figures. Again, asking the right question for the wrong reason, he calls Tang Hao's contention that Wang Zongyue received the four-line "Sparring Song" in Chen Village and elaborated it to six lines "pure nonsense." Certainly, too much of Tang's case rested on the shaky assumption of Wang Zongyue's historicity and Chen Wangting's creation of taijiquan, but Li Shirong's chief complaint is that Tang's dating would make Wang Zongyue two centuries too late to receive a direct transmission from Zhang Sanfeng. To weaken the Zhang Sanfeng authorship claims, Tang and Gu had cited the many parallels between the taiji classics and Zhou Dunyi's *Explanation of the Taiji Diagram* and the fact that this work was not published until 1757, too late to have influenced a Ming Daoist. Li, however, counters that Zhou received the interpretation of the taiji symbol from the Daoist immortal Chen Xiyi, and that it was independently handed down in Daoist circles until it reached Zhang Sanfeng, who was then inspired by it to create taijiquan. As further proof, he cites a diagram attributed to Wang Zongyue's student Jiang Fa and reproduced in handwritten manuscript form in a 1990 issue of *Wudang* magazine. He does not attempt to explain why this "Ming" manuscript is written in simplified characters. The release of old handwritten manuscripts attributed to the likes of Chen Changxing (Luchan's teacher), Wang Zongyue, and Jiang Fa is another aspect of the pseudo-scholarship phenomena. These are written in classical Chinese and contain large doses of Daoist jargon and channel theory, but the appearance of Western biomedical terms such as "blood pressure" (*xueya*) does not inspire confidence in their authenticity. If they were authentic, however, it would require us to throw out the existing corpus of "classics" and accept a whole new canon.

In the end, all of this can teach us nothing about the true origins of taijiquan, but a great deal about the contemporary intellectual milieu in China. Sima Nan, who has made it his personal mission to expose qigong cults, referred to the leader of one such cult as the "patriarch of a new religion," and Zhang Honglin refers to the qigong craze as "heretical cults." Taijiquan, at least, has had the decency to deify its invented ancestor and not a living exponent, but even socialism was not immune to the "cult of personality." Since it is difficult to use a capitalist discourse to undermine a "communist" regime that is privatizing everything in sight, and democracy is not perceived as a sure cure for poverty and corruption, it seems that only a religious movement can rally sufficient passion and numbers to challenge the regime. Taipings and Boxers are good examples from not so distant history, and the new Zhang Sanfeng cult shows that *Falun Dafa* (lit. "Great Law of the Wheel of Law"; also, *Falun Gong*) is not an isolated case. Paralleling the emergence of ethnic and provincial localism, defining "Chineseness" is no longer exclusively a monopoly of the state, but can be contested by special interests. Daoism wedded to taijiquan is once again resurrected as a carrier of Chineseness in an era of global economic integration. Instead of seeing this subculture as appealing to those who are left behind in the race to the modern, it may be that spiritual aspirations based on the work ethic of earned immortality through strenuous effort, and conferring a profound and secure sense of Chinese identity, may comport with the new entrepreneurial spirit in China in the same way that the Protestant ethic supported the rise of capitalism in the West. Certainly, for the subculture of Zhang Sanfeng cultists, the reconstruction era image of the proletarian "iron man" has given way to the myth of the Daoist immortal/warrior. Daoist chauvinism should never be underestimated, and we need only remind ourselves that some Daoist apologists have claimed that Buddhism sprang from seeds planted by Laozi when he rode westward on his ox.

Conclusion

The little old ladies in China's parks today, with their taiji swords, sly smiles, and twinkling eyes, probably care little about taiji's role in national self-strengthening, reviving the martial spirit, surviving Manchu, Western, and Japanese imperialism, post-modern religious fundamentalism, the ultimate fighting art, taiji tourism, cultural exports, identity politics, or the construction of masculinity. The martial arts politics of hard versus soft, of idealist versus materialist, and of scholarship versus religion will not trouble them. They probably never have fantasies about Zhang Sanfeng or dream of the God of War.

For non-Chinese practitioners, many of these concerns will likewise be irrelevant, but that does not mean that they do not have preconceptions of their own. Chinese ideologues have thought of taiji as a secret weapon in the epic struggle of civilizations; Western practitioners are more likely to think on the scale of the schoolyard or mean streets. Chinese martial arts missionaries and merchants in the West may see taiji as a vehicle for raising respect for Chinese culture, but Western practitioners are more likely to see their involvement in purely personal terms, consciously or unconsciously caught up in warrior dreams, the search for surrogate father figures, intentional community building, physical therapy, orientalism, or alternative spirituality.

Practitioners East and West have been polarized by the issue of whether taijiquan is essentially a fighting art or a moving meditation. Some are deadly serious about taiji as a fighting art, and some feel that taiji is to fighting what dance is to sex: ways to play with aggressive or erotic energy without going over the top. The Daoist-taiji connection in China was painstakingly constructed, and fiercely contested, but presented to the West as a fait accompli.

Leaving politics and scholarship aside, is taijiquan a good vehicle for exploring Chinese culture, and in particular Daoism? In China, the question has always been what did Daoism do for taiji, but in the West we can also ask what did taiji do for Daoism? How does it compare with language, history, literature, the arts, and travel as ways of exploring Chinese culture? To the extent that letting go, non-action, relaxing, egolessness, and no-mind must be actualized to perform the solo form or succeed in self-defense, dabbling in literature and philosophy cannot compare. Performance with the body is the essence of ritual and the reason why taijiquan can be such a powerful delivery system for the insights of Laozi, Zhuangzi, and the inner alchemists. As a theoretical model for explaining why taiji succeeds, Daoist philosophy is a perfect fit, but that does not mean that Daoism invented taiji—Pao Ding the butcher was not a Daoist.

Taijiquan and Daoism Glossary

Bian Renjie	卞人傑	Jiang Fa	蔣發
caizhan	採戰	jin	勁
Cantongqi	參同契參	jing	靜
Chang Naizhou	萇乃周	li	力
Chen Changxing	陳長興	liangzhi liangneng	良智良能
Chen Fake	陳發科	lingkong faqi	凌空發氣
Chenshi taijiquan tushuo	陳氏太極拳圖説	Li Shirong	李師融
Chen Qingping	陳清苹	Li Xiyue	李西月
Chenshi jiapu	陳氏家譜	Li Yaxuan	李雅軒
Chenshi jiasheng	陳氏家乘	Li Yiyu	李亦畬
Chen Wangting	陳王庭	Li Zhaosheng	李兆生
Chen Weiming	陳微明	Lu Dimin	路迪民
Chen Xin	陳鑫	Lü Dongbin	呂洞賓
"Da dao lun"	大道論	Ma Yuannian	馬原年
dianxue	點穴	Ma Yueliang	馬岳梁
Dong Yingjie	董英傑	ming	命
Du Yuanhua	杜元化	Neijia quanfa	內家拳法
Feng Zhiqiang	馮志強	Neijing	內經
Gan Fengchi	甘鳳池	Ningbo fuzhi	寧波府誌
Ge Hong	葛洪	Pan Jianping	潘建平
Gu Liuxin	顧留馨	Pao Ding	庖丁
Guoji lunlue	國技論略	Qi Jiguang	戚繼光
Guo Tiefeng	郭鐵峰	Qingshi gao	清史稿
Hao Weizhen	郝微真	Quanjing	拳經
He Hongming	何鴻明	"Quanjing zongge"	拳經總歌
Huang Baijia	黃百家	Shaolin quanshu mijue	少林全數秘訣
Huangting jing	黃庭經	Shaolin zongfa	少林宗法
Huang Zongxi	黃宗羲	Shao Yong	紹雍

Bibliography — English

Alter, J. (1992). *The wrestler's body: Identity and ideology in north India.* Berkeley: University of California Press.

Ames, R. (1993). The meaning of the body in classical Chinese thought. In T. Kasulis, et al., (Eds.), *Self as body in Asian theory and practice* (pp. 149-56). Albany, NY: State University of New York Press.

Ames, R. (1993). On the body as ritual practice. In T. Kasulis, et al. (Eds.), *Self as body in Asian theory and practice.* Albany, NY: State University of New York Press.

Benthall, J. and Polhemus, T. (Eds.). (1975). *The body as a medium of expression.* London: Allen Lane.

Blacking, J. (Ed.). (1977). *The anthropology of the body.* New York: Academic Press.

Brownell, S. (1995). *Training the body for China: Sports in the moral order of the People's Republic.* Chicago and London: University of Chicago Press.

Csordas, T. (Ed.). (1994). *Embodiment and experience: The existential ground of culture and self.* Cambridge: Cambridge University Press.

Donohue, J. (1994). *Warrior dreams: Martial arts and the American imagination.* Westwood, CT: Bergin and Garvey.

Donohue, J. (1993). The ritual dimension of karate-do. *Journal of Ritual Studies* 7(1): 105-24.

Frank, A. (2000). "Kung fu fighters without history: Imagining tradition with Shanghai taijiquan players." Paper presented at Association for Asian Studies 2000 Annual Meeting as part of panel "Creating, Selling, and Remembering Martial Arts in Modern China."

Herman, D. (2000). "The commodification of chi: Remythologizing martial arts in the 20th century." Paper presented at Association for Asian Studies 2000 Annual Meeting as part of panel "Creating, selling, and remembering martial arts in modern China."

Hobshawn, E. and T. Ranger (Eds.) (1983). *The invention of tradition.* Cambridge: Cambridge University Press.

Kasulis, T., et al (Eds.). (1993). *Self as body in Asian theory and practice.* Albany: SUNY Press.

Kierman, F. and Fairbank, J. (Eds.) (1973). *Chinese ways in warfare.* Cambridge: Harvard University Press.

Kotkin, J. (1993). *Tribes: How race, religion, and identity determine success in the new global economy.* New York: Random House.

Law, J. (Ed.). (1995). *Religious reflections on the human body.* Bloomington:

Indiana University Press.

Miura, Kunio (1989). The revival of qi: Qigong in contemporary China. In Kohn, L., and Yoshinobu, S. (Eds.), *Taoist Meditation and Longevity Techniques*, pp. 331-363. Ann Arbor: Center for Chinese Studies, The University of Michigan.

Morris, A. (2000). "National skills: Martial arts and the Nanjing state, 1928-1937." Paper presented at Association for Asian Studies 2000 Annual Meeting as part of panel, Creating, selling, and remember martial arts in modern China.

Oakes, T. (1998). *Tourism and modernity in China.* London and New York: Routledge.

Oakes, T. (August 2000). China's provincial identities: Reviving regionalism and reinventing 'Chineseness.' *The Journal of Asian Studies* 59(3): 667-692.

Ong, Aiwa (1999). *Flexible citizenship: The cultural logics of transnationality.* Durham, NC: Duke University Press.

Otis, T. (1994). The silenced body—The expressive Leib: On the dialectic of mind and life in Chinese cathartic healing. In T. Csordas, (Ed.), Embodiment and experience: The existential ground of culture and self. Cambridge: Cambridge University Press.

Rankin, M. (1986). *Elite activism and political transformation in China.* Stanford: Stanford University Press.

Rogoski, R. (2000). "Fists of Fury" or the Jingwu hui before Bruce Lee. Paper presented at Association for Asian Studies 2000 Annual Meeting as part of panel Creating, Selling, and Remembering Martial Arts in Modern China.

Seidel, A. (1970). A Taoist immortal of the Ming dynasty: Chang San-feng. In W. de Bary (Ed.), *Self and Society in Ming Thought.* New York: Columbia University Press.

Sharf, R. (1995). Whose Zen? Zen Nationalism Revisited. In J. Heisig and J. Maraldo, (Eds.), *Rude awakenings* (pp. 40-51). Honolulu: University of Hawaii Press.

Sivin, N. (1996). *Medicine, philosophy and religion in ancient China: Researches and reflections.* Alsershot, Great Britain: Variorum.

Stephenson, N. (1995). *The diamond age, or "A young lady's illustrated primer."* New York: Bantam.

Sutton, N. (1993). Gongfu, guoshu, and wushu: State appropriation of the martial arts in modern China. *Journal of Asian Martial Arts* 3(1): 102-14.

Tanaka, S. (1994). Imagining history: Inscribing belief in the nation. *Journal of Asian Studies*, 1: 24-44.

Victoria, B. (1997). *Zen at war*. New York: Weatherhill.

Wile, D. (2007). *Zheng Manqing's uncollected works on taijiquan, qigong, and health, with new biographical notes*. Milwaukee, WI: Sweet Ch'i Press.

Wile, D. (2000). *T'ai-chi's ancestors: The making of an internal martial art*. New City, NY: Sweet Ch'i Press.

Wile, D. (1996). *Lost t'ai-chi classics from the late Ch'ing dynasty*. Albany, NY: State University of New York Press.

Wile, D. (1985). *Cheng Man-ch'ing's advanced t'ai-chi form instructions, with selections on meditation, the I ching, medicine, and the arts*. Brooklyn, NY: Sweet Ch'i Press.

Wile, D. 1983. *Tai-chi touchstones: Yang family secret transmissions*. Brooklyn, NY: Sweet Ch'i Press.

Wile, D. (1982). *Master Cheng's thirteen chapters on t'ai-chi ch'uan*. Brooklyn, NY: Sweet Ch'i Press.

Xu Ben (1998). 'Modernity to Chineseness': The rise of nativist cultural theory in post-1989 China. *Positions: East Asia Cultures Critique*, 6(1): 203-37.

Xu Jian (1999). Body, discourse, and the cultural politics of contempory Chinese qigong. *The Journal of Asian Studies*, 4: 961-91.

Yuasa Yasuo. (1987). *The Body: Toward an eastern mind-body theory*. Albany: State University of New York Press.

Zito, A. and T. Barlow, (Eds.). (1994). *Body, subject, and power in China*. Chicago: University of Chicago Press.

Bibliography — Chinese

Chang Naizhou (1936). *Changshi wuji shu* (Chang Naizhou's writings on martial arts). Xu Zhen (Ed.). Taiwan reprint, n.p., n.d. Xu Zhen preface, 1932; first published 1936.

Chen Bin (1989). Taijiquan yu daojiao guanxi bian. (Questions regarding the relationship between taijiquan and Daoism). *Zhonghua wushu* 5: 26-27.

Chen Changxing (1994). Taijiquan shida yaolun (Ten treatises on taijiquan). *Wuhun* 8: 44-45.

Chen Jifu (1935). *Chenshi taijiquan rumen zongjie* (General introduction to Chen family taijiquan). Taibei: Hualian Publishing House, 1980 reprint.

Chen Weiming (1925). *Taijiquan shu* (The art of taijiquan). Hong Kong: Xianggan Wushu Publishing House, n.d.

Chen Xin (1933). *Chenshi taijiquan tushuo* (Introduction to Chen family taijiquan). Hong Kong reprint: Chen Xiangji shuju, 1983; Author's preface, 1919; first published 1933.

Feng Fuming (1989). Guanyu 'taijiquan yuanliu' wenti de tongxin (An exchange of letters on the question of taijiquan's origins). *Wudang* 4: 22-24.

Fu Chengjiang (1991). Wudangquan yu Zhongguo gudai zhexue sixiang de guanxi (The relationship between Wudang boxing and ancient Chinese philosophy). *Wudang* 1: 35-38.

Fu Zhenlun (1983). Cong wushu de lishi fazhan kan wushu de shehui zuoyong (Looking at the social function of the martial arts from the point of view of their historical development). *Henan tiyu shiliao* 3: 1-4.

Gu Liuxin and Tang Hao (1963). *Taijiquan yanjiu* (Studies on taijiquan). Hong Kong: Bailing Publishing House.

Gu Liuxin and Tang Hao (1982). *Taijiquan shu* (The art of taijiquan). Shanghai: Jiaoyu Publishing House.

Guo Tiefeng (1999). Qigong dadao taijiquan (Qigong, the great dao, and taijiquan). *Jingwu* 3: 28-29.

Han Kang (1998). Taijiquan zaikao cong Wang Zhengnan shengping (Reexamining taijiquan from the point of view of the life of Wang Zhengnan). *Wudang* 4: 12.

Hao Chin (1988). Lun lishi shang tiyu yu zongjiao de guanxi (On the historical relationship between physical education and religion). *Tiyu wenshi* 4: 12-18.

Hao Chin (1990). Lun Zhongguo wushu dui daojiao wenhua de rongshe (On the absorption of Daoist culture into the martial arts). *Tiyu wenshi* 1: 7-11.

Hao Wen (1987). Zhouyi yu taijiquan shu (The *Yijing* and taijiquan). *Wulin* 3: 4-5.

He Hongming (1997). Yangshi taijiquan dingxing qian ceng de daomen gaoren zhidian (Yang Luchan received instruction from a Daoist before finalizing his form). *Wudang* 6: 34-35.

Huang Baijia. Neijia quanfa (Art of the internal school's boxing methods). *Zhaodai congshu*, Vol. 163.

Huang Zongxi. *Nanlei ji* (Collected works of Huang Zongxi). Shanghai: n.p., n.d.; photoreprint of 1680 edition.

Huang Zhaohan (1989). *Mingdai daoshi Zhang Sanfeng kao* (A study of the Ming dynasty Daoist Zhang Sanfeng). Taipei: Xuesheng Shuju.

Jiang Bailong, et al. (Eds.). (1992). *Wudangquan zhi yanjiu* (Studies on Wudang

Boxing). Beijing: Beijing Tiyu Xueyuan Publishing House.

Jin Yiming (1936). Guoshu ying yi rujia wei zhengzong (Confucianism should be the true philosophy of the martial arts). *Guoshu zhoukan* 3: 156-57.

Kang Gewu (1983). Tansuo quanzhong yuanliu de fangfa (Methods in tracing the origins of martial arts styles). *Zhonghu wushu* 1: 43-44.

Kong De (1997). Zhang Sanfeng "Dadao lun" shuzhu (Zhang Sanfeng's "Treatise on the Great Dao" with annotations). *Wudang* 1: 39-41; 2: 38-40; 3: 42-44; 4: 37-39; 5: 38-39; 6: 38-39; 7: 40-41; 8: 39-40; 9: 35-36; 10: 38-40.

Li Jifang (1997). Chen Wangting 'yici' bian (Problems in Chen Wangting's 'Posthumous Poem'). *Tiyu wenshi* 3: 33-35.

Li Jinzhong (1989). Taojiao sixiang dui taijiquan de yingxiang (The influence of Daoism on taijiquan). *Zhonghua wushu* 1: 32-33.

Li Shirong (1998). Wang Zongyue, Wu Yuxiang liang quanpu de bijiao yu jianbie (Comparing and contrasting the martial arts manuals of Wang Zongyue and Wu Yuxiang). *Zhonghua wushu* 9: 10-13.

Li Shirong (2000). Zhang Sanfeng bu shi taiji bizu (Zhang Sanfeng is not the creator of taijiquan). *Jingwu* 6: 26-27.

Li Shirong (1999). 'Taijiquan lun' zhuzuo beijing ji niandai kaozheng (A study of the background and date of the author of the "Treatise on taijiquan"). *Wulin* 7: 4-10.

Li Zhaosheng (1998). Zhang Sanfeng zushi shengxiang xiezhen (Creating the holy image of master Zhang Sanfeng). *Wudang* 2: 6-8; 3: 4-5.

Li Zhaosheng (1996). Taijiquan shi xianxia jiandao fanhua yu su de xiuwei (Taijiquan is a spiritual practice of martial adepts that has filtered down to the common people). *Wudang* 8: 6-9.

Li Zheng (1999). Shilun taijiquan de 'shu' he 'dao' (A preliminary discussion of the technique and dao of taijiquan). *Wudang* 7: 19-20.

Li Zejian (1995). 'Taijiquan lun' de zuozhe shi shei? (Who is the author of the "Treatise on taijiquan?") *Wuhun* 2: 51.

Liang Qichao (1916). Zhongguo zhi wushidao (Japanese bushido). *Yinbingshi congshu*, Vol. 7. Shanghai: Commercial Press.

Liu Changlin (1987). Zhongguo gudai yinyang shuo (Ancient Chinese theories of yin and yang). *Wuhun* 4: 20-21.

Liu Junxiang (1988). Gudai zheli yu lunli dui Zhongguo wushu xingcheng he fazhan de yingxiang (The influence of ancient philosophy and ethics on the formation and development of Chinese martial arts). *Tiyu wenshi* 5: 51-56.

Lu Dimin (1996). 'Chenshi jiapu' pangzhu kao (A study of the annotations to the "Chen family geneology"). *Wudang* 9: 48-49.

Lu Dimin and Zhao Youbin (1992). *Yangshi taijiquan zhengzong* (Orthodox Yang style taijiquan). Beijing: Sanqin Publishing House.

Lu Zhaoming (1987). Wushu zhong de yinyang wuxing shuo (The yin-yang and five phases theories in the martial arts). *Tiyu wenshi* 4: 5-6.

Ma Guoxiang (1997). Caotan taijiquan de quanwai gong (A discussion of non-pugilistic elements in taijiquan). *Wuhun* 2: 12-13.

Ma Hong (1991). Taiji taijitu taijiquan (Taiji, the taiji symbol, and taijiquan). *Wulin* 2: 22-23.

Ma Hong (1998). Shilun daojia sixiang dui taijiquan de yingxiang (A preliminary discussion of the influence of Daoist thought on taijiquan). *Wudang* 3: 27-31.

Ma Yuannian (1998). Taijiquan he rujia sixiang (Taijiquan and Confucian thought). *Shaolin yu taiji* 11: 32-33.

Meng Naichang (1987). Taijiquan de zhexue jichu (The philosophical foundations of taijiquan). *Tiyu wenshi* 4: 47-52.

Meng Naichang (1990). Laozi yu taijiquan (Laozi and taijiquan). *Wudang* 1: 28-33.

Mo Chaomai (1999). Rujia wenhua yu wush (Confucian culture and the martial arts). *Zhonghua wushu* 5: 38-40.

Mo Chaomai (1997). Baguazhang, taijiquan shi sheji zhi qingmo zhuwang kao (An examination of the involvement of the Manchu princes in the history of baguazhang and taijiquan). *Wuhun* 5: 43-44.

Niu Jia (1987). Taijiquan yu weiren zhi dao (Taijiquan and ethics). Zhonghua wushu 5: 43.

Qi Jiguang n.d. *Jixiao xinshu* (New and effective methods in military science). Ma Mingda (Ed.). Beijing: Renmin Tiyu Publishing House, 1986.

Qian Timing (1997). Taijiquan lilun tanyuan (An exploration of the theory of taijiquan). *Wudang* 5: 17-21.

Shan Zhongzi (1998). Guben 'taijiquan midian' (An ancient "Secret taijiquan classic"). *Wudang* 5: 21-22.

Sheng Qing. Zai fugu zhong qiu de jietuo (In search of an escape from the revivalist movement). *Wuhun* 3: 13.

Song Zhijian (1970). *Taijiquan xue* (The study of taijiquan). Taibei: Song Zhijian.

Su Jingcun (1989). Liang Qichao de shangwu sixiang yu minzu tiyu de xingjue (Liang Qichao's military thinking and the development of national physical education awareness). *Tiyu wenshi* 3: 22-25.

Su Xiaoqing (1988). Kang Youwei de tiyu sixiang ji qi chengyin (Kang Youwei's views on physical education and their background). *Tiyu wenshi* 1: 49-52.

Su Xiongfei (1975). Kongzi de tiyu kechenglun fangfalun ji qi pingjia (The role of physical education in Confucius' curriculum, its methodology, and an evaluation). *Tiyu xueshu yantaohui zhuankan:* 33-39.

Sun Lutang (n.d.). *Taijiquan xue* (The study of taijiquan). Hong Kong: Xianggang Wushu Publishing House, n.d.; preface dated 1919.

Tan Benlun (1991). Lun Wudang Songxi pai neijiaquan (On the Wudang Songxi lineage of the Internal School). *Wudang* 1: 15.

Tang Hao (1958). Jiu Zhongguo tiyu shi shang fuhui de Damo (Falsifications concerning the role of Bodhidharma in the history of Chinese physical education). *Zhongguo tiyu shi cankao ziliao*, Vol. 4.

Tang Hao (1935). *Neijiaquan de yanjiu* (A study of the internal school). Hong Kong: Unicorn Press, 1969 reprint.

Tian Yongpeng (1988). Chuantong wushu yu gudai zongjiao yishi qiantan (A preliminary examination of traditional martial arts and ancient religious consciousness). *Tiyu wenshi* 3: 28-29.

Tong Xudong (1994). Sun Jianyun dashi fangtan lu (An interview with master Sun Jianyun). *Wuhun* 10: 36-37.

Tong Xudong (1990). Sun Jianyun xiansheng tan 'sanquan heyi' (Master Sun Jianyun discusses the unity of the three internal martial arts). *Jingwu* 12: 23.

Wang Huai (1992). Taojiao yangshengshu yu taijiquan (Daoist health practices and taijiquan). *Wudang* 4: 23-24, 26.

Wang Xinwu (n.d.) *Taijiquanfa chanzong* (The principles of taijiquan). Xian: Shaanxi Renmin Publishing House, 1959 (reprint); Hong Kong: Taiping shuju, 1962 reprint.

Wang Xian (1988). Yinyang xueshuo yu Zhongguo chuantong wushu (Yinyang theory and traditional Chinese martial arts). *Tiyu wenshi* 2: 3, 21.

Wang Zixin (1988). Taijiquan zheyuan tan (An exploration of the philosophical sources of taijiquan). *Zhonghua wushu* 2: 11-13.

Wu Gongzao (1935). *Taijiquan jiangyi* (Commentaries on taijiquan). Shanghai: Shanghai Bookstore, 1991.

Wu Tunan (1991). *Wu Tunan taijiquan jingsui* (The essence of Wu Tunan taijiquan). Beijing: Renmin Tiyu Publishing House.

Wu Tunan (1984). *Taijiquan zhi yanjiu* (A study of taijiquan). Hong Kong:

Commercial Press.

Wu Tunan (1928). *Taijiquan* (Taijiquan). Hong Kong: Jinhua Publishing House, n.d.

Wu Zhiqing (n.d.) *Taiji zhengzong* (Orthodox taijiquan). Shanghai: Shanghai Bookstore, 1986 (reprint); Hongkong: Jinhua Publishing House, n.d.

Wu Wenhan (1995). Yitiao yu Chengou wushu youguan de shiliao (An historical item on Chen Village martial arts). *Wuhun* 11: 17.

Xi Yuntai (1985). *Zhongguo wushu shi* (The history of Chinese martial arts): Beijing: Renmin Tiyu Publishing House.

Xu Zhen (1930). *Guoji lunlue* (Summary of the Chinese martial arts). Shanghai: Commercial Press.

Xu Zhen (1936). *Taijiquan kaoxin lu* (A study of the truth of taijiquan). Taipei: Zhenshanmei Publishing House, 1965 reprint.

Yan Han (1999). Taijiquan lishi shang zhi mi (A mystery in taijiquan's history). *Wulin* 8: 10-11.

Yang Chengfu (1931). *Taijiquan shiyong fa* (Self-defense applications of taijiquan). Taibei: Zhonghua Wushu Publishing House, 1974 reprint.

Yang Chengfu (1934). *Taijiquan tiyong quanshu* (Complete principles and applications of taijiquan). Taibei: Zhonghua Wushu Publishing House, 1975 reprint.

Yang Honglin (1996). Jianshu Zhang Sanfeng neidan lilun (A brief exposition of the theory of Zhang Sanfeng's inner elixir method). *Wudang* 4: 28-32.

Yang Shaoyu (1990). Shendao xuanxue yu wushu yundong (Mysticism, metaphysics, and the martial arts movement). *Wudang* 3: 21-30.

Yang Yong (1987). Xian you neijiaquan hou you Zhang Sanfeng (The internal school predates Zhang Sanfeng). *Tiyu wenshi* 4: 16.

Yu Jianhua (1986). Taijiquan lilun de zhexue jichu chutan (A preliminary discussion of the philosophical foundations of taijiquan theory). *Zhejiang tiyu kexue* 3: 10-13.

Yu Zhijun (1991). Wudang neijiaquan de quanli shi kexue haishi xuanxue (Is Wudang internal boxing theory science or metaphysics?). *Wudang* 6: 35-37.

Zeng Qingzong (1988). Taiji daojiao he shui: taijiquan zheli tansuo (Taiji, Daoism, and water: Tracing the philosophical principles of taijiquan). *Wulin* 4: 42-43.

Zeng Zhaoran (1960). *Taijiquan quanshu* (Complete taijiquan). Hong Kong: Youlian Publishing House.

Zhang Ruan (1988). Neijiaquan dashi Zhang Songxi shengping bianwu

(Correcting errors in the biography of internal school master, Zhang Songxi). *Tiyu wenshi* 4: 28-30.

Zhang Weiyi (1988). Shixi rujia sixiang dui chuantong tiyu fazhan de yingxiang (An analysis of the influence of Confucian thought on the development of physical education). *Tiyu wenshi* 1: 39-43.

Zhang Xuanhui (1984). Wuou youdu jue yichan neijia que you liuluquan (A unique legacy: the Internal School's Six Paths still exits). *Wulin* 5: 32.

Zheng Qing (1998). Taiji shuzhen (The truth about taijiquan). *Shaolin yu taiji* 4: 40-41.

Zheng Zhenkun (1988). Lun Huang Zongxi dui Zhonghua wushu de lishi gongxian (On Huang Zongxi's historical contribution to Chinese martial arts). *Tiyu wenshi* 6: 46-48.

Zhi Zi (1996). Fo Ru Dao huxiang yingxiang manyi (A discussion of the mutual influence of Buddhism, Confucianism, and Daoism). *Shaolin yu taiji* 4: 9.

Zhou Linyi (1975). Laozi sixiang yu tiyu benzhi (Laozi's thought and the nature of physical education). *Tiyu xueshu yantaohui zhuankan* 1: 40-48.

Zhou Weiliang (1991). Dui jianguo hou wushu shehui kexue lilun yanjiu de sikao. (An examination of social science theory in the martial arts since the founding of the People's Republic). *Wuhun* 4: 7-8.

Zunwozhai zhuren (n.d.). *Shaolin quanshu mijue* (Secrets of Shaolin boxing).

· 8 ·

Yoga Alchemy in Taijiquan

by Greg Brodsky, Lic. Ac.

Balance

I always ask beginning students what they want from their investment in taijiquan. Without hesitation, the great majority of them talk about "balance." They don't mean physical balance, although that, much to the appreciation of our older students, is guaranteed to improve with practice over time. They are looking for a way to *inner* balance—a method for increasing their ability to weather the storms in their lives without being knocked around too much, without losing their emotional footing so often and paying such tremendous costs for their mistakes, or perhaps a way to avoid draining all their reserves of energy and optimism into endeavors or obsessions that consume them then disappear like last night's fleeting dream.

This is the kind of balance you need when your love seems betrayed, or your career collapses, or you realize that your religion was an exploitive hoax. Our beginning students hope that something in taijiquan will teach them how to develop the skill, strength, and resilience with which they can meet the rest of their days with greater wisdom.

"No problem," I tell them with a wry smile. But they usually recognize the irony behind my smile.

Yes, this is a tall order. Such inner development, achieving a state of internal balance, does not come naturally to most people. It follows years upon years of admitting mistakes, facing the consequences of our actions, cultivating consciousness, giving unqualified forgiveness, and softening... all the time softening our stance. When the time comes for each of us to find out what we are made of, the difference between drawing it all together or missing the opportunity as if it were not there comes from the degree to which we have tuned our inner resources to be prepared for a transformation we cannot predict. If we meet such a moment in balance, we transcend something we no longer need, embrace something we once feared, and emerge as our greatest self.

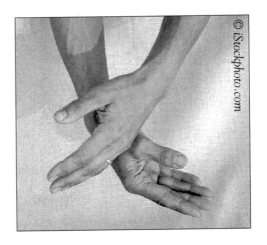

Self-Tuning

In any arena of human endeavor, those of us who can tune ourselves while in motion, who can learn to relax, to listen, to become hypersensitive to early warning signs and navigational signals of many kinds, and to make critical course corrections without having to stop or pause when the heat is on will have a better chance of prevailing than those who invested themselves in a single skill, or method, or technique. It is not too much to say that the better we can be at tuning ourselves, the better will be our entire experience of being.

This critical element becomes increasingly important as we mature, especially as we approach our later years. Maturing toward mastery, self-tuning enables us to continue dissolving unhealthy tensions in our bodies and rigidity in our minds. Relaxing more deeply year after year, we can enjoy finding a little more space in our aging joints, space that gains value with every passing day. Having learned to enhance our *gaze* (I address this below) and quiet our emotions, we can see more clearly, even as our eyes grow older. We feel with greater sensitivity, respond more appropriately, and waste less energy on nonsense. These enhancements come to us because we tune ourselves like a musician tunes her instrument, day after day after day.

Eventually, if our practice touches the whole of our lives, we learn how to experience inner peace. The *gongfu* (martial arts effectiveness) in our art gives us a unique kind of pleasure, but the result of years of practice is the state of mind/body that we bring to our families, colleagues, and communities. We are tuning our very *state of being*. In this sense, for us, taijiquan is a yoga as well as a martial art.

This chapter began because I wanted to improve my ability to tune my aging body/mind, to keep my balance during unusually difficult times, and to help our students do the same. Since 1964, taijiquan has humbled me, confounded me, and challenged every instinct with which I grew up. Now seeking to better understand my blind spots, I sat back from my typical approach to training (do more) and took a long look at several of my colleagues whom I admired. These weren't people who never fell out of balance, nor were they taiji purists who counted on this one art to have given them everything they needed to know. We shared the realization that, while our chosen art might have *all* the answers, we weren't necessarily able to assimilate them. For us, an occasional look through another lens could be useful. One close friend, a farmer, a great boxer, and an accomplished musician, found his most profound respite and reflection in music. Another, whose push-hands skills always amazed me, also took hatha yoga classes several times a week. We agreed that sometimes the best way to see inward is to look through a completely different set of principles. I decided that comparing the principles of taijiquan and hatha yoga would be interesting. Several taiji teachers told me later that, for them, taijiquan and yoga had blended into a single discipline.

In examining that "single discipline," I had to separate these two schools of thought and then compare their components, their principles, and their methods. To be fair minded, I put the gongfu aspect aside to focus on the straightforward benefits to body, mind, and spirit—but, I could not put it far. Among the great treasures hidden within taijiquan, there are those that can only be realized by "tasting bitter," "investing in loss," and "listening to and following one's opponent," gifts that come in ways one cannot imagine until something goes still and silent inside. I touch on these below.

But first, I had to ask the question: how does taijiquan measure up as a yoga?

Hatha Is Yang-Yin

The word *yoga* means "union" (Devereux, 1998: 5). The practice of hatha yoga attempts to create the union of polar opposites in the way that taijiquan seeks to establish a dynamic balance between yin and yang. *Ha* means "sun" (yang) and *tha* means "moon" (yin), so "sun-moon union" loosely translates to "yang-yin reconciliation."

Both philosophies have articulated the characteristics of each end of the polarity in great detail. Distinctions such as hot-cold, male-female, aggressive-passive, strong-weak, hard-soft, to name a few, build a picture of opposites that could form a bipolar, tripolar, or multiple-polar matrix. In some cases, the poles could represent the tendency to do good, the tendency to do evil, and the tendency to transcend both good and evil. In another example, every being lives with the simultaneous urge toward agency (coming into being) and dissolution (going out of being), while equally being driven toward progressing and regressing. The key point is that each individual can manifest relatively more of one pole than another and, in so doing, be out of balance.

Both philosophies consider the reconciliation of these grand cosmological opposites to be essential milestones in a person's development. According to yogic philosophy, for example, until we achieve this reconciliation, we exist in a state of inner conflict. Perceiving an "either-or" world, we cling to one end of an eternal polarity and reject the other, it's opposite. Unable to experience the greater whole, we feel exposed, isolated, and unsafe. The very act of being makes us anxious because we try to fit in (to be "good") while desperately separating ourselves from essential parts of our true selves (that which we consider "bad") and the world in which we live.

Both the Chinese and Indian philosophies consider the dynamic balance of their polarity to be essential for life, but at some point the idea of balancing energies that one considers positive (sun, yang) and negative (moon, yin) loses its moral attribution. Positive does not mean "good," with negative being "bad." They are simply describing characteristics, such as a positive electrical charge, for example, or negative (empty) space. In a balanced system, they compliment each other, support each other, and become each other. Too much of either destabilizes that balance, giving the practitioner the task of finding ways to restore it, just as does the natural universe in its incomprehensibly dynamic ways.

After years of pattern-challenging and consciousness-raising practices, we can realize that our separation is an illusion. Through this awakening, we achieve union within ourselves, and with it, union with the world. Through personal reflection and practice over time, dualism becomes oneness. The yogi surrenders to the whole and realizes Brahman. The Daoist resonates with the very movement of the universe. The "Way that cannot be named" can be lived, and so we live it.

The taiji practitioner learns to become quiet enough to "hear" the intentions of others, sensitive enough to feel forces previously unknown to us, and still within ourselves, whether our bodies are in motion or not. Our practice settles and expands our sphere of thought until we experience both the polarity and the unity of yin and yang. The words of the great sage, Laozi, inspire us: "To the mind that is still, the whole universe surrenders."

Both yoga and taijiquan offer breathing and movement exercises, meditative processes, behavioral injunctions, and other disciplines that propose to cultivate such expansive stillness; both seek to prolong the life and enhance the health of the practitioner. For adepts of these systems, the path is one of inner transformation that eventually leads to outer transformation.

Compatible Elements

Looking into the cosmologies that support these concepts, our scope expands beyond the specific disciplines of yoga and taijiquan. The five-element models described below form the bedrock of Chinese and Indian cultures, for example, most importantly where their systems of medicine are concerned.

Within, and perhaps as products of this balancing process, both cultures also discern the emergence of five essential elements. The Chinese model identifies wood, fire, earth, metal, and water (Veith, 2002); the Indian model identifies, respectively: ether, fire, earth, air, and water (Devereux, 1998: 6). Exploring the comparative depths of these elements is beyond the scope of this chapter, but understanding how the yogic use of them can apply to taiji practice proves handy. The names and foci of the yogic elements are as follows (Devereux, 1998: 5-7):

Drushti (space, ether)
Asana (structure, alignment, earth)
Vinyasa (quality of movement, water)
Pranayama (quality of breathing, air)
Bandha (energetic transformation, fire).

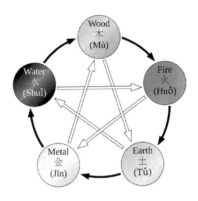

And here we gain a useful tool: the yogic blueprint for a balanced practice. With this blueprint in mind, let's look at how one organizes and approaches the work we do. I invite you to examine your own practice to identify comparable, conflicting, and perhaps missing elements. If you find something missing in your practice, or you see the opportunity to refine a part of it, please note that the only requirement is that you make your enhancements responsibly.

Drushti: The Mind's Eye

Drushti, the element of ether, determines the context in which one lives. In the Chinese medical model, it is loosely analogous to wood, which governs an individual's capacity for planning and decision making. *Drushti* describes a person's attention, intention, or awareness. Your drushti determines the "gaze" through which you perceive your situation and your purpose in it.

When playing taijiquan through the yogic gaze, one can find oneself easing into a growing awareness of previously unknown paths to self-realization. For those who have strong instincts about martial arts, and who require of themselves the achievement of extraordinary levels of skill and awareness, such achievement might define the completion of the path. Still others, as has been the case for me, can find themselves drawn to the inner and outer game of metaphorical combat and disciplined playfulness that martial arts provide. We interact in the spirit of bear cubs rolling on a grassy hillside, enthusiastically locked in each other's jaws

154

while never intending to cause real harm. Like other natural animals, we want to develop our innate survival tools and abilities; as culturally conscious and moral animals, we wish to never need to use these tools in earnest.

If, as a student, one's mind's eye focuses on cultivating playfulness and mutual well-being, he is already practicing taijiquan as a yoga, an exercise of union. This drushti creates agility in the body/mind and, because you take yourself lightly, enables you to move lightly on your feet.

I find that in taiji form practice, a yogic frame of mind enables a person to learn while simultaneously enjoying a healthy sense of self-acceptance. One must begin with what is, and this acceptance or recognition of that which already is provides a foothold for learning. Rather than complacency, such a willing acceptance can promote exquisite attention to what you are doing as you become aware of your body's position in space—head, hands, feet, hips, shoulders, knees, elbows—as well as spinal alignment, quality of movement, breathing, thinking, and in time, the intrinsic energies moving through your body. The demands you place on yourself, while dedicated to drawing out the best in you, are gentle, even loving. Such is the nature of most yogic drushti.

Push-hands becomes play. © *iStockphoto.com*

By contrast, one might approach yoga or taijiquan or any other practice as a performance art. The competitor in us wants to win; the insatiable ego wants to be recognized, to outdo others while insisting that we continually surpass our previous performances. We expect to "get it" quickly, and are dismayed —instead of intrigued—to find that our chosen path might confound us for years, maybe forever. We bring pressure into our practice that, while generally useful in excellence-oriented contexts like sports, can be the very opposite of our long-term purpose in choosing taijiquan over other paths.

As students, excellence demands that we walk a thin line between driving ourselves and cultivating ourselves. The compulsively driving mindset, a psychological characteristic of many educational and cultural traditions, assumes that the student is lazy or mediocre by nature and must be whipped into shape, driven to develop, forced out of the comfort zone. The teacher has to push, even humiliate, each student into stepping beyond his limitations, and as students we sustain the harsh voices of our most vociferous teachers in our heads long after they are gone. Instead of union, we try to learn through constantly self-evaluating pressure.

In this state of mind, our mistakes embarrass us. We try learning while feeling self-conscious about not knowing what we don't yet know. Our practice is never good enough, and the eye of our teacher makes us feel vulnerable and inadequate.

SIDEBAR

Imagine yourself at taiji camp for the next five days on the Big Island of Hawaii (circa mid -1990s). The hot, tropically aromatic air melts your very bones as you find yourself among fifty or so practitioners of various ages and skill levels coming from different parts of the world to dedicate six hours a day to practice taijiquan. Some are just beginning. For others, this is their fifteenth camp and a chance to mix it up with some good boxers.

The teacher is Grandmaster William C. C. Chen, who is showing the group how to throw a punch. An astonishing boxer, he demonstrates a straight right several times with explanations, then asks the students to try it themselves. Surveying the group for a few moments, he picks a fifty-something woman who clearly has no martial arts background and asks her to show what she can do.

"We're looking at Shirley" (not her real name), he says. "Go ahead."

Shirley punches, appropriately looking like she's never done this before.

"Yes!" Chen exclaims with enthusiasm. "That's great. Now, just do it again and drop your shoulder."

Shirley punches again, dropping her shoulder.

"Yes!" he exclaims again, with enough enthusiasm to get her grinning. "Now, just bend your knee."

She punches; he acknowledges and corrects her. She punches again; he encourages her more and makes additional corrections. By the time she has thrown a dozen punches, she is starting to get the idea. He never tells her no.

Chen is not telling her that she is doing it right. He is saying yes to her effort. It takes courage for her to try in front of this group, to learn something foreign to her background, to listen to feedback and apply it. He knows what he is doing: he is building her spirit, expanding the space in which she can learn, cultivating drushti.

Many ancient schools fostered this approach with the intent of toughening and enabling students to overcome their weaknesses. In their most philosophical contexts, they taught that real victory was "victory over the self." In their more misguided moments, they simply taught ways to brutalize self and others under the rubric of learning.

After thirty or forty years of training, I find, one comes to realize that victory over the self is an illusion. We might develop tremendous discipline, but we conquer nothing within. Real maturity means discovering what we are, coming to peace with it, and thus ending the war with ourselves. Inner peace enables us to cultivate better habits and prune away our worst ones in sustainable, low-maintenance ways. Instead of fighting with ourselves, we learn how to genuinely update our ideas and behaviors. In the process, we reconcile with our inner demons, and when we do, they can become allies, willing participants in our continued evolution as human beings.

Cultivation is the operant word here. Inner cultivation occurs as a slow, nurturing, loving, fearlessly honest process of realizing how we think and behave, responding more sensitively to the world around us, recognizing the feelings that attune us to our true nature and purpose in life, trusting these feelings, optimizing them, and acting on them. The mind that watches and directs this process is our drushti.

Asana: Sound Structure

Asana means "alignment" (Devereux, 2006: 7-8), and all the postures that yogis practice are called *asanas*. These are not static poses, but instead dynamic combinations of opposing and balancing forces that send spirals of energy through the body to awaken its cellular intelligence.

In the yoga of taiji, we find cellular intelligence in the *jin* (intrinsic strength) (Zhang, 2006: 14-20), which is the very nature of our cells expressing their collective power. We become adept at sensing and cultivating this natural power when we relax, focus our minds on a single action, and take that action in ways that *passively* compress our bones and tissues along a line that starts in our foot or feet, runs through our legs and spine, and ends in one hand, both hands, or the other foot—when kicking, for example.

The line being compressed is the line of *jin*, the internal hardness hidden within an envelope of softness. Our *jin* is the intrinsic strength of our cells. Compare this to untrained *extrinsic* effort, or *li* (raw force), which is not part our cells' essential nature and so demands actively exerted force.

We find our *jin* by becoming mentally quiet and physically relaxed enough to feel the strength that is already there, then moving in ways that optimize that strength. This means we let our *jin* influence our movements in the way that the heft of a sword influences how we wield it. In this state of attentiveness, we "listen" to the *jin*.

Walking, standing, and jumping provide straightforward ways to understand this idea. Your body knows just how much you need to tense your muscles in order to stand. If you jump, you don't have to think about how much to tense and which muscles to tense when you land. Your body already knows (personal communications with William C. C. Chen).

This is somatic intelligence, *jin* in action. Translating the body's wisdom from these mundane actions into the elegant movements of taijiquan marks the beginning of cultivating internal power. Recognizing that the practitioner doesn't move by magic, but by physiology and kinetics in which muscles contract to pull bones into place, we can pay attention to what actually happens in our bodies when we move with coordinated ease and power. Our attentiveness enables us to blend metaphor (what we are thinking) and mechanics (what we are doing) in ways that make us move more competently. While for years we might focus primarily on relaxing, we don't relax completely; if we did, we would fall to the floor in a heap. We relax selectively so unnecessary tensions dissolve and necessary ones occur, giving us essential hardness with no sense of effort.

You can't cultivate this hardness—internal *jin*—by trying to be strong.[1] Effort and force lead to excessive tension that masks the very power you are trying to discover. Instead, you cultivate internal *jin* by aligning your body—guided by gravity—so that in each moment you can feel the force vector that extends from your substantial foot through your *dantian* (lower abdomen) and spine to your hands, relaxing everything that is not on this vector, and activating it through thought.[2]

Your interpretation of a movement—a push, for example—defines the line of force being delivered; your *qi* (energy) then gets your body parts in place to deliver it. But qi, being directed by your conscious mind, is distinct from the *jin* you discover.

In this sense of discovery, you cultivate *jin* by getting out of its way. As you align the firm line from foot to hand in each taiji movement, you think of the line being passively compressed as it joins its real or imaginary target. Instead of feeling effort when you apply a move, you have the sensation of letting go. This sensation occurs whether you are uprooting a training partner or practicing form on your own.

To sense this in solo practice, students are advised to imagine applying the moves to an actual person; your intention to "apply" the move will define a line of firmness between your root and your virtual opponent. Don't tense this line; just visualize it connecting your foot to your contact point—your hand, for example—in a way that compresses you into your foot. Relax, and let the firmness reveal itself to you.

To find the same sensation in push-hands, which requires seriously tempering your ego, imagine your partner to be a mirror of yourself: your beneficent twin. Instead of trying to uproot an opponent, imagine letting your beneficent twin compress you from time to time—no effort, no winning, just joining your twin and aligning yourself between him and the earth so his mass compresses you into the earth. When your twin gets uprooted, it's not because you try to do anything; you just happen to be there when he gets overly ambitious and uproots himself.

Zheng Manqing taught, "Play form as if you were with an opponent; play push-hands as if you were alone" (Lowenthal, 1993: 109). While this practice takes imagination and can prove psychologically challenging, it awakens your awareness of the *jin* that embodies your somatic intelligence. The hard within the soft awakens the bright within you where your brightness might have been clouded by social conditioning.

Alone or with others, you cultivate *jin*—as well as qi—by practicing congruency in your thoughts and actions. This means you do one thing at a time and pay attention to what you are doing. Practicing congruency reduces habitual, chronic tensions and extends through your taiji forms, interactive exercises, everyday societal encounters, personal behaviors, and even meditations. As you learn to calm your busy thoughts, you can develop single-mindedness. As you learn to move with gravity-aligned balance, you can discover the power waiting in your cells. In time, you find that single-minded—unconflicted—*jin* is intelligent in the sense that it keeps you from doing stupid things to yourself; it is always economical, simple, respectful of physical reality, and present, if you can become mentally and emotionally still enough in yourself to feel it.

Yoga calls this stillness "dying in the posture" (Devereaux, 1998: 16). Yogis put themselves into shapes that challenge their chronic tension patterns, then stay there for a specified time based on the body's needs and capacity to respond. When the body/mind has let go, one has "died" in the posture. Waiting for this moment takes tremendous discipline and loving, noncompetitive, unambitious patience. The taiji version occurs during standing-posture practices and in the moment of release that happens in form practice each time you reach the peak or energized part of a movement (Brodsky, 2005).

While much of yoga's somatic opening occurs on a mat, yogis also rely on standing postures to bring the body back together. Master practitioner Godfrey Devereux (1998: 27) declares, "Of all the yoga postures the most important for awakening somatic intelligence are the standing postures." The yogic idea of alignment in these postures is opened, connected, engaged, energized, and balanced.

Vinyasa: The Quality of Movement

Most people think of yoga practice as "stretching." This superficial idea misses the point in the same way as interpreting taijiquan's goal to be "relaxing." While we relax to release and open our joints (sung), we do so to enliven and empower our movement. In the way that yoga seeks to awaken the body/mind, taiji seeks to generate extraordinarily powerful, effortless action that leads to the same awakening: the awakening of our inner power and the cultivation of the spirit that gives us life.

Yogis can hurt themselves by forcing themselves to stretch, and taiji players hurt themselves by forcing themselves into stances that are too low for them, tucking the tailbone too far forward, forcing or resisting during push-hands, and a myriad of creatively destructive ways of holding knees, necks, and shoulders in unnatural positions. Over time, practicing your forms with some yogic consciousness can change those habits and bring about therapeutic changes.

Vinyasa means "to place [the body] in a special way" (Devereaux, 1998: 44-45). It refers to the order in which one practices asanas and the quality of movement and breathing with which the practitioner goes from posture to posture. Here yoga more resembles qigong than taijiquan, because rather than just gaining the outcome of enhancing qi, the "quan" part also seeks to develop martial arts effectiveness and the personal equanimity that comes from dealing with one's ego in relationship to others, friendly or otherwise.

Neither yoga nor taiji is about posing. In the same way that the asanas are dynamic states of balanced forces, the taiji "postures" are snapshots of moments in a continuum, conveniently named so we can talk about them. No two pushes are alike, just as no two situations are alike. We just think we are doing the same movement over and over again, when in fact we are setting up a series of actions and "launching" them without knowing precisely where and how they will complete themselves by connecting with each other. When you are present in your practice, despite the fact that you have done a move a thousand times, each time is unique.

Nor is taiji form about moving slowly, but rather about operating in such a way that we optimize our most powerful natural energies: life force, intrinsic strength, spirit. We learn to sense and cultivate those energies when we develop a state of mind that approaches mindfulness meditation. This could involve fast or slow or no movement, but it just happens that we find it easier to cultivate this state when we move slowly. Once awakened, our mindfulness can be exercised no matter what we are doing.

With these different intentions noted, the principles of movement are similar: relax and open the joints; elongate your spine from the top of your head downward; surrender to gravity in both your vertical alignment and in your movements; link your movements together in such a way that each movement creates the one that follows; breathe freely; focus; be present.

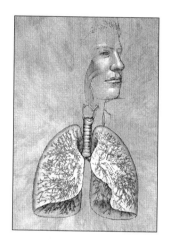

Pranayama: The Quality of Breathing

Pranayama is the practice of energetic regulation through the breath (Devereux, 1998: 56-59). *Prana* is essentially qi, and *ayama* loosely translates to "extension." Practices for personal transformation through energetic regulation date back thousands of years, and all consider breathing to be a primary tool.

Some yoga employs audible breathing (*ujjayi*), which, because of the throat tension it requires, is not recommended when practicing taijiquan. According to classical instructions, taijiquan calls for slow, silent, long, and thin breathing during form practice, and, often, the use of compressive sound during fast movement or qigong. Exceptions abound to this statement, so it appears here as a rule of thumb. Whatever the practice, students are advised to breathe freely.

In applying yogic principles to taiji practice, we confront the chicken/egg question: which comes first, the breath or the movement? If we momentarily set aside the schools that say, "Don't worry about the breathing; it will come naturally," or, "Just breathe naturally," we can ask what, precisely, the relationship is between breath and movement in taiji.

Conscious "compression breathing" provides each movement with a pneumatic boost (Brodsky, 2004: 37-44). William Chen taught me about compression breathing, but my personal conviction about it comes from studying breathing when doing physical work (gaining added power), when my spine became injured (bracing the spine), with older people (helping them move), when we are surprised or excited (we inhale), when passively relaxing (even my dog lets out a sigh when he is done running around), and when decompressing and compressing my body in practicing taiji form.

With compression and decompression in mind, I contend that the chicken—that is, the movement—comes first and dictates how one should breathe. My favorite test is to ask a person to go from a seated to a standing position and experiment with different ways of breathing: inhaling, exhaling, or holding. The reader is invited to try these and see which way feels most natural and powerful.

But let's ask the opposite question: if you were standing and suddenly your knees caved in as if you were passing out, what would happen to the air in your body? Would your lungs fill with air? Or would the air in your lungs be expelled without your trying to exhale? Then, if you caught yourself halfway down, how would you breathe to regain yourself?

I propose that you would lose air as you fell and inhale as you recovered, catching your breath as you caught yourself from further falling. By testing breathing in a wide variety of situations, experimental and practical, I have come to the conclusion that natural breathing in the slow practice of taiji form means inhaling when you extend your body and exhaling when you flex it (Brodsky, 2004).

Zheng Manqing's instructions on the matter of breathing during form practice consist of inhaling when the arms move up and away from the body and exhaling when the arms move down and close to the body (Cheng and Smith, 1966: 11). William Chen is much more explicit about using the breath, instructing his students to exhale just before each energized move (the "applied" part) in the form, and to gently inhale to compress the dantian as the move is energized ("applied"). When demonstrating fast punches, he almost always lets out a sound, releasing compressed air, but not simply exhaling.

Along with compression breathing, one can practice a useful technique that we'll call here "expansion" breathing. I discovered this method while doing standing/rooting practices. As do many schools, we often hold postures for a few minutes while we adjust our form and settle into the substantial foot to deepen our root. Periodically, I notice some people cringing instead of sinking. It is as if they are trying to get shorter, smaller, to occupy less space in the room. Once noticing this cringing, and making sure it wasn't just from burning thighs or other pain, I began to spot the same pattern in their form and push-hands practice as well.

This cringing is especially noticeable in tall people, who might have developed the habit while trying to fit in while growing up in a shorter world. Others, with the idea of "sinking the elbows" or "depressing the chest" (Liao, 1990) sometimes pinch their armpits inward, which contracts their torsos across the line of the clavicles. The corrective response is to "smile" across the clavicles, widening them to take their full, allotted space.

This gentle clavicular smile remedies the armpit pinch, and relieves the upper torso and neck of much of their tension. Instead of depressing the chest, one empties the chest of its grip on itself and lets the clavicles roll back into the chest and the scapulae drop until the whole shoulder girdle finds its natural angle of repose. This enables the idea of suspending the head from above to extend into the upper torso. Long spine, wide frame, released chest.

Expansion breathing adds to this relief and extends the mental space that a person occupies. To practice it, I suggest playing a round of your form and stopping at each posture for three full breaths. Imagine that each inhalation expands your entire body in all directions, as if you were filling up like a balloon, becoming one or two sizes larger. Then imagine that each exhalation emanates from your pores, so you "exhale through your skin" as you let gravity relax you. Expand on each inhalation and release on each exhalation. Stay in each posture for three breaths, adjusting into your most satisfying alignment; then move on. As you breathe, affirm to yourself that you are taking all the space to which your body/mind is entitled.

Esoterically described, we might call this practice "expanding your field of qi." In simpler terms, I think of it as just a wholesome exercise that changes how you see and feel your body.

Bandha: Energetic Transformation

Bandha means "seal" or "lock" (Devereaux, 1998: 48-51), and, like the gates and internal channels of taijiquan and Daoist meditation, the bandhas of yoga are thought to open certain energetic doors in the body while closing others. Daoist alchemists and yogis consider these to be spiritual openings through which one can enter a dimension of the self that can't be accessed by ordinary means. Because traditional explanations can prove arcane, we are best served here by comparing only a few generalized commonalities of yogic and Daoist models and keeping our terms as anatomical as possible.

Also, a disclaimer: Esoteric schools sometimes offer promises that few, if any, fulfill. Immortality is hard to come by; tantric transmutation into pure white light might require batteries; astonishing stories of physics-defying qi rarely pass the test of public scrutiny. When delving into the transformative aspects of taijiquan, the less magical is often more reliable.

With that caveat in mind, exercising the bandhas in your taiji practice can liberate considerable energy. One can introduce oneself to this practice by standing comfortably with feet parallel to each other and wide enough apart that they could be hanging off your hips. Too wide will create unnecessary tension, and too narrow might feel unstable. Bend your knees.

Begin by thinking about the highest point of the top of your head. This is the area from which you "suspend your head from above," the crown chakra in yoga, the upper dantian (*ni wan*) in Daoist yoga, and associated with the *bai hui* point (hundred meetings) of the energetic governing vessel that runs up the back of your body in Chinese medicine (Lu, 1970: 124). Here you maintain part of your attention, a sense of lightness, as if you were being pulled upward and gently reaching upward at the same time.

Building on this light feeling, gently expand the space between the base of your skull and the back of your neck. When you "empty the chest and raise the back," a sense of fullness and softness begins here. At the same time, imagine your whole head floating upward, away from your shoulders, which gently drop to your sides. Think, "Long spine, wide frame."

Extending your attention downward to the seventh cervical vertebra, which is known as the "great hammer" in Chinese medicine, relax the base of your neck. This is the posterior portion of the yogic throat chakra, which is thought to be the seat of your personality. Here the forward curve of your neck starts to become the backward curve of your torso, and so presents a stress point, a gate that closes

164

with tension and that you can open through gentle elongation. Preparing to yawn without actually yawning is a simple way to open this point.

The backward curve of your torso switches to a forward curve at the twelfth thoracic vertebra, the last one that has ribs attached to it, and the backdrop to your heart chakra and middle dantian. If you think of the space between this vertebra and the one below it, the first lumbar, gently expanding, the curve naturally flattens an appropriate amount and this gate opens. Do this without effort by breathing into your heart. A good sigh goes a long way here.

The lumbar spine meets your sacrum around the level of your hips. By continuing to think about elongation, you can align this juncture a little more vertically. As implied earlier, you don't need to tuck your sacrum as much as to drop it so you feel like you are sitting. This promotes the release of your *kua* (hip crease) and flattens your low back.

Now hang there, sensing your lower dantian and thinking, "Long spine, wide frame." The only work you should feel is in your thighs, depending on how much your knees are bent. Your spine is elongated and its gates are open: minimal tension, optimal alignment with gravity, and the energy can flow.

From here continue to widen your frame. This occurs at your shoulders and hips. Imagine your shoulders falling to the sides as you "smile" across the clavicles. Simultaneously rotate your clavicles back toward your shoulder blades as you gently release those blades to fall down toward your posterior ribs. "Plucking up the back" (Liao, 1990) doesn't mean becoming slightly hunchback; it means filling the back with qi by thinking about the energy that runs up the back as you align and relax. Lengthening your spine and smiling into your shoulders as just described facilitates this movement of energy.

Regarding the pelvis, some schools advocate contracting the perineum. I find this unnecessary, being an appropriately neurotic product of Western culture, and prefer to smile across the pelvis instead. This pelvic smile automatically causes the pelvic floor to raise a little, gently engages the abdominal muscles, and supports the lumbar spine better than trying to contract the perineum. To find the smiling muscle, which is the *transversus abdominus*, just bend forward a tiny bit and press your thumbs into your abdomen at a point halfway between your navel and pubic bone, about two inches to each side. Press firmly; then cough. The muscle you feel contracting when you cough is the *transversus*.

Now smile across the clavicles and pelvis, and you have a "wide frame."

"Long spine, wide frame" provides the basis of taiji's bandha, or transformational energy work. The next step is in the spirals and gates in your arms and legs.

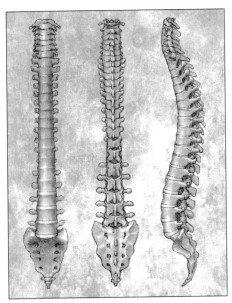
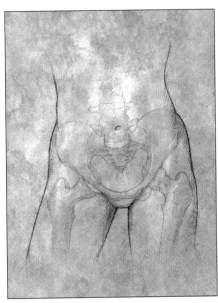

Bandhas and Gates

Taiji literature describes the "nine pearls" namely: the wrist, elbow, shoulder, ankle, knee, hip, and the three major curves of the spine (Wile, 1983: 107). These are the gates that open to release qi and close to contain it. When open, the gates decompress, elongate, and loosen as we have just done. When closed, the gates compress and express the firmness of *jin*. In taiji practice, your task is to align your skeleton so the force vector that passes through your body travels easily and naturally from foot to hand, connecting the gates in between. Peter Ralston describes it as "lining up the billiard balls."

Having long been confused by the descriptions in the classics—e.g., what do I do with "When the outer gate opens, the inner gate closes?"—I have often found myself experimenting with the gates. Once I realized that *jin* felt different from qi, statements like "Where there is no qi, there is pure hardness" started to make sense. Distinguishing more sensitively between substantial and insubstantial helped as well, as did a deeper surrender to gravity. Bottom line: relax everything that is not working, direct your qi with thought instead of effort, and listen to the *jin*.

Once your spine is aligned and elongated, next come the spirals that move through your arms and legs as you energize your moves. The task is to feel the lines through which *jin* and qi operate.

To sense these lines, take any comfortable stance and focus your mind on one leg. As you feel that foot pressing into the floor, *imagine* that you are gently rotating your lower leg inward (toward the center of your body) along the axis of your bones while rotating your upper leg outward to the sides. Don't move anything, most notably your knees; just add a little tone to the lower leg one way (inward) and to the upper leg the other way (outward). Gently tense the tiniest bit with these rotations in mind.

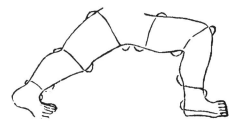

Spirals indicate energy flow through
the legs, depicted in Chen Xin's book,
Illustrated Explanation of
Chen Family Taijiquan, from the 1920's.

It will feel like you are creating dynamic tension in your leg, and you are. This engages the bandha of the leg, exciting your qi more than you would by just standing there. Try it in one leg, then the other, then both. Then try it in different stances.

You can easily overdo it, so make it more of an attitude than an effort. Stand still and feel what energetics these rotations produce; then see if you can feel those energetics as they extend up your spine to the top of your head. Take your time; relax your torso as much as possible so you can feel the soft flow of qi that passes through your sinews and the hard line of *jin* that passes through your bones.

While maintaining "long spine, wide frame," extend your awareness into your arms. Taking any posture that you typically practice, gently rotate the upper arm outward as you torque the lower arm in toward your thumb. No movement is necessary, just the very subtle tension that comes with intention. The energetics of this intention end up in your thumb, index finger, and middle finger.

Now, connect your feet to your hands. Feeling the pressure of your feet on the floor, the spiral inward of your lower legs, the spiral outward of your upper legs, the feeling of firmness (*jin*) that signals the connective power of your legs, pelvis, and spine, your long spine and wide frame that reaches to the top of your head, the outward spiral of your upper arms, and inward spiral of your lower arms, you are connected.

Breathe deeply and enjoy this feeling. You are experiencing the yoga of taijiquan. When practicing form, one can concentrate on any aspect of this experience or none of it, since the natural spirals and alignments will come in time.

As we have seen, these yogic ideas—drushti, asana, vinyasa, pranayama, and bandha—can become embedded into your skill set as gentle enhancing nuances. Your gaze can be gentle and clear, your alignment sound, movement fluid, and breathing easy as you cultivate transformative energies throughout your body, preparing pathways for your spirit to rise. And rise, it will.

Notes

[1] This refers to *nei jin*, the subtler internal strength. *Wai jin*, which is related to physical power, can be developed through muscle-oriented training.

[2] According to taiji principles, one leg is always more weighted and in higher tonus, therefore more "substantial" than the other. Power emanates from the substantial leg as the practitioner visualizes the intended move being applied.

References

Brodsky, G. (August 2004). "Compression breathing," *Tai Chi Magazine*, 28(4): 37-44.

Cheng, M. and Smith, R. (1966). *T'ai Chi: The "supreme ultimate" exercise for health, sport, and self-defense*. Boston: Charles Tuttle Publishing.

Devereux, G. (1998). *Dynamic yoga*. Toronto, ON: HarperCollins/Thorsons Publishing.

Liao, W. (1990). *Tai chi classics*. Boston: Shambhala Publishing.

Lowenthal, W. (1993). *There are no secrets: Professor Cheng Man-ch'ing and his tai chi chuan*. Berkeley, CA: North Atlantic Books.

Lu K'uan Yu (1970). *Taoist yoga*. London: Rider and Co.

Veith, I. (2002). *The yellow emperor's classic of internal medicine*. Berkeley, CA: University of California Press.

Wile, D. (1983). *T'ai chi touchstones: Yang family secret transmissions*. Brooklyn, NY: Sweet Ch'i Press.

Yang, J. (1999). *Taijiquan: Classical Yang style*. Boston: YMAA Publication Center.

Zhang, Y. (April 2006). "Zhang Yun on the use and development of jin in taiji, Part II." *T'ai Chi Magazine*, 30(3): 14-20.

index